Macmillan
English

Tina Thoburn
Rita Schlatterbeck
Ann Terry

SERIES **E** ®
Macmillan English

Macmillan Publishing Co., Inc. / New York   Collier Macmillan Publishers / London

ACKNOWLEDGMENTS

The publisher gratefully acknowledges permission to reprint the following copyrighted material:

"Secret Places" from *Secret Places* by D. J. Arneson. Copyright © 1971 by Don Jon Arneson.

"Bus Ride" from "Ferry Ride" from *City Child* by Selma Robinson. Copyright 1931, © 1959 by Selma Robinson. Reprinted by permission of Holt, Rinehart and Winston, Publishers.

"Song of the Train" from *Far and Few* by David McCord. Copyright © 1952 by David McCord. Reprinted by permission of Little, Brown and Company in association with the Atlantic Monthly Press.

"Tom Sawyer—Fence Washer" by Steven Otfinoski. Copyright © 1982 by Macmillan Publishing Co., Inc.

"I Can Be . . ." from the book *I Can Be . . .* by A. K. Roche. Copyright © 1967 by A. K. Roche. Published by Prentice-Hall, Inc., Englewood Cliffs, New Jersey.

"Blaze Finds the Trail" by C. W. Anderson. Reprinted with permission of Macmillan Publishing Co., Inc. from *Blaze Finds the Trail.* Copyright © 1950 by Macmillan Publishing Co., Inc., renewed 1978 by Phyllis Anderson Wood.

"Chinese Brush Painting" from *The Zoom Catalog* by WGBH Educational Foundation. Copyright © 1972 by WGBH Educational Foundation. Reprinted by permission of Random House, Inc.

"The Surprise Party" reprinted with permission of Macmillan Publishing Co., Inc. from *The Surprise Party* by Pat Hutchins. Copyright © 1969 by Pat Hutchins. *The Surprise Party* by Pat Hutchins is published in the United Kingdom by The Bodley Head.

Illustration Credits:
Howard Berlson, Helen Cogancherry, Olivia Cole, Mac Conner, Len Ebert, Creston Ely, Fred Harsh, Tom Herbert, Marilyn Janovitz, Hima Pamoedjo, Jan Pyk, Helen Rodewig, Jose Reyes, Mario Stasolla, Pat Stewart, John Wallner, Lane Yerkes

Photography Credits:
Erik Arnesen 34/35, 146/147
Ingbert Grüttner vi1, 68/69, 106/107, 182/183, 218/219
Ringling Brothers & Barnum and Bailey Circus 254/255

Wyeth, Anderew, *Christina's World* (1948). Tempera on gesso panel, 32¼ x 47¾. Collection, The Museum of Modern Art, New York. Purchase 256
Cover photo: © Norman Snyder

Parts of this work were published in the original edition of SERIES E: Macmillan English.

Macmillan Publishing Co., Inc.
866 Third Avenue, New York, New York 10022
Collier Macmillan Canada, Ltd.

Printed in the United States of America
ISBN 0-02-246320-8

TABLE OF CONTENTS

UNIT 1

Grammar and Related Language Skills   Sentences I . . .2–17

Practical Communication   Time-Order Paragraph 18–27

Checking Skills 28–29

Creative Expression 30–33

UNIT 2

Grammar and Related Language Skills   Nouns I 36–55

Practical Communication   Descriptive Paragraph 56–63

Checking Skills 64–65

UNIT 5

UNIT 6

UNIT 7

UNIT 8

Grammar and Related Language Skills

Sentences
Three Kinds of Sentences
Subject Parts and Predicate Parts
Punctuation for Sentences

Practical Communication

Using the Parts of a Book
Writing a Time-Order Paragraph

Creative Expression

A Story

Learning About Sentences

You use words every day. You put words together to explain your ideas to other people. Some groups of words do not make sense. They do not tell enough to show a complete idea. Other groups of words make sense. They state a complete idea.

A **sentence** is a group of words that states a complete idea.

- Read these two groups of words.

The tiger hides behind a tree.   The tiger.

The first group of words states a complete idea. It tells about a tiger, and it tells what the tiger does. The first group of words is a sentence.

- Read the second group of words again. It names a tiger, but it does not tell what the tiger does. The second group of words is *not* a sentence.

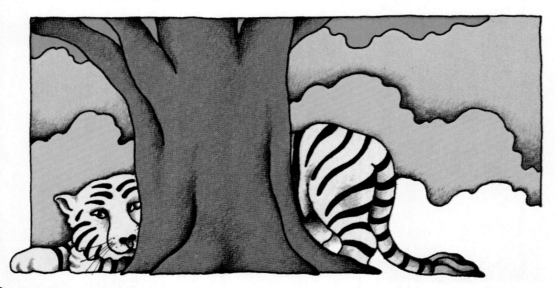

Talk About It

Read the groups of words in each pair. Which group of words is a sentence?

1. Many animals.
   Many animals live at the zoo.

2. Two bears.
   Two bears sat on a rock.

Skills Practice

Read the groups of words in each pair. Write each group of words that is a sentence.

1. A turtle.
   A turtle crawled to the fence.

2. The raccoons washed their food.
   The raccoon.

3. The penguins.
   The penguins hopped into the pond.

4. An owl.
   An owl hooted to a bird.

5. A deer drank water.
   A deer.

6. Some birds.
   Some birds flew to the nest.

Sample Answer 1. A turtle crawled to the fence.

Word Order in Sentences

The words in a sentence must come in an order that people can understand. The words state a complete idea when they are in the right order.

- Read the groups of words in each pair. Which groups of words are in the right order to make a sentence?

Likes hay the elephant.   Three deer nibbled grass.
The elephant likes hay.   Nibbled three grass deer.

The words in a sentence must be in an order that makes sense. You must put the words in an order that says what you want to say.

- Look at this picture that Jim drew. He wrote a sentence about his picture. Which of these two sentences do you think he wrote?

The rabbit eats a carrot.
The carrot eats a rabbit.

Talk About It

Look at the order of the words in each pair of sentences. Which sentence tells about the picture?

1. A frog swam in the lake.
   The lake swam in a frog.

2. A fly swallowed the frog.
   The frog swallowed a fly.

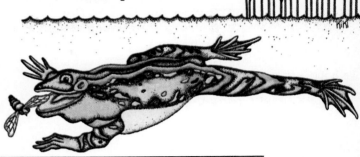

Skills Practice

Read each group of words. Write the group of words that is in the right order to make a sentence.

1. Climbs a the tree monkey.
   The monkey climbs a tree.

2. A bear swam in the pond.
   The in pond swam bear a.

3. A child fed the lamb.
   The fed a lamb child.

4. To zoo the is fun trip a.
   A trip to the zoo is fun.

Look at the order of the words in each pair of sentences. Write the sentences that tell about the picture.

5. A fox ran around a tree.
   A tree ran around a fox.

6. The tree climbed a raccoon.
   A raccoon climbed the tree.

7. A branch flew from the robin.
   The robin flew from a branch.

Sample Answers 1. The monkey climbs a tree. **5.** A fox ran around a tree.

Three Kinds of Sentences

You use different kinds of sentences every day. Sometimes you use sentences to *tell* something. Sometimes you use sentences to *ask* something. Sometimes you use sentences to show strong feeling.

A **telling sentence** is a sentence that tells something.

A **question sentence** is a sentence that asks something.

An **exclamation sentence** is a sentence that shows strong feeling.

● Read each sentence about the picture. Is it a telling sentence, a question sentence, or an exclamation sentence?

The hen eats corn.   Two children feed the raccoon.
Do you see a door?   How nicely the cat plays!

- Look at the picture. Make up one telling sentence about the monkey. Make up one question sentence about the rabbits. Make up one exclamation sentence about the chicken.

Talk About It

Read each sentence. Is it a telling sentence, a question sentence, or an exclamation sentence? Give a reason for each answer.

1. Do you have a pet?
2. I have a monkey and a cat.
3. Is it hard to take care of a monkey?
4. The monkey gets into trouble.
5. What a bad monkey it is!

Skills Practice

Read each sentence. Write **telling** if it is a telling sentence. Write **question** if it is a question sentence. Write **exclamation** if it is an exclamation sentence.

1. We saw an elephant at the zoo.
2. Was the elephant very big?
3. What a huge elephant it was!
4. It splashed water on us.
5. Next we saw some bears.
6. How hungry the bears looked!
7. Did you see any monkeys?
8. We saw many monkeys.
9. Have you ever been to a zoo?

Sample Answer   1. Telling

Beginning and Ending Sentences

When you talk, your voice gives signs that help people understand you. You take a short rest at the end of each sentence. Your voice is often higher at the end of a question. Your voice can express strong feeling.

- Listen while your teacher reads this story. Listen to hear when each sentence begins and when it ends. Try to hear which sentences are question sentences. Which sentence expresses strong feeling?

How cold the dragon felt! Winter was coming. It had no warm place to stay. What could it do?

The dragon hunted and hunted. At last it found a dry cave.

The dragon was still cold. How do you think it warmed up the cave?

When you write sentences, you need to show where each sentence begins and where it ends.

Use a **capital letter** to begin the first word of every sentence.

Some snakes sleep all winter.
Do cows sleep all winter?
How funny my cat looks!

- Look at the story again. How do the sentences begin?

Use a **period** (.) at the end of a telling sentence.

Many horses sleep standing up.

Use a **question mark** (**?**) at the end
of a question sentence.
How do other animals sleep?

Use an **exclamation mark** (**!**) at
the end of an exclamation sentence.
What a sleepy dog that is!

● Look at the story again. How do the sentences end?

Talk About It

Look at the beginning and end of each sentence.
What special signs are missing in each sentence?

1. i have a pet duck.
2. Can you see it

3. how funny it is!
4. i will feed it now

Skills Practice

Some special signs are missing in each sentence.
Write each sentence correctly.

1. my dog was lost.
2. where did you find him?
3. He was under a bush

4. What was he doing
5. he was sleeping
6. how happy he was!

Writing Sentences

Pretend that the zoo has a new kind of animal.
It is part raccoon and part duck.

1. Write a question sentence about the animal.
2. Write a telling sentence about the animal.
3. Write an exclamation sentence about the animal.

Sample Answer **1.** My dog was lost.

Skills Review

Read the groups of words in each pair. One group in each pair is a sentence. It states a complete idea. Write the sentence in each pair.

1. The children fed the ducks.
   The children.

2. Some monkeys.
   Some monkeys ate bananas.

3. An owl.
   An owl fell asleep.

4. A goat walked past.
   A goat.

Read the groups of words in each pair. Write the groups of words that are in the right order to make a sentence.

5. A dog into the ran yard.
   A dog ran into the yard.

6. A dog followed Ben home.
   Ben a dog followed home.

7. Ben fed the dog.
   Fed the dog Ben.

8. Ate dog the.
   The dog ate.

Look at the order of the words in each pair of sentences. Write the sentence that tells about the picture.

9. Carmen jumps into the water.
   The water jumps into Carmen.

10. The pool fell into her shoes.
    Her shoes fell into the pool.

11. A fish catches Peter.
    Peter catches a fish.

Look at each sentence. Write **telling** if it is a telling sentence. Write **question** if it is a question sentence. Write **exclamation** if it is an exclamation sentence.

12. Mae and Nancy went to the pet store.
13. How big the store is!
14. Have you ever been to a pet store?
15. Did you want to buy a pet?
16. The children wanted to buy the kittens.
17. What a sweet kitten that is!

Look at the beginning and end of each sentence. Some special signs are missing in each sentence. Write each sentence correctly.

18. the bear has warm fur.
19. What color is the fur
20. It is brown
21. did you hear that noise?
22. what a big bear it is!

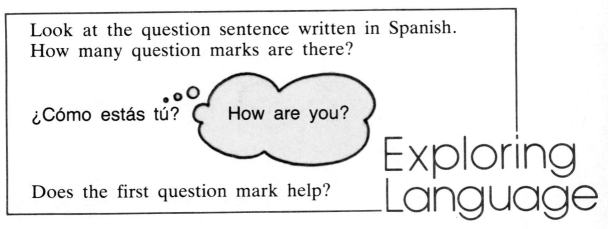

Look at the question sentence written in Spanish. How many question marks are there?

¿Cómo estás tú? How are you?

Does the first question mark help?

Exploring Language

Parts of Telling Sentences

You know that a telling sentence is a group of words that states a complete idea. Every telling sentence has two parts. Each part does a special job in the sentence. The two parts work together to tell a complete idea.

The **subject part** of a sentence names whom or what the sentence is about.

The **predicate part** of a sentence tells what action the subject part does.

- Read each sentence. What is the subject part? What is the predicate part?

The class | went to the circus.
The children | saw many things.
The ponies | raced around the ring.
Lions | roared.
The clowns | jumped out of a tiny car.

Talk About It

Read each sentence. Is the part in the box the subject part or the predicate part?

1. The class | watched a magic show.
2. A flower | turned into a white rabbit.
3. The white rabbit | turned into a bird.
4. The bird | flew away.

Skills Practice

Read each sentence. Look at the part in the box. Write **subject** if it is a subject part. Write **predicate** if it is a predicate part.

1. The children | saw a funny circus act.
2. A clown | brought some monkeys into the ring.
3. A red monkey | took the clown's hat.
4. A brown monkey | took the clown's shoes.
5. The funny clown | chased them.

Write each sentence. Draw a line between the subject part and the predicate part.

6. Joe gave his pups a bath.
7. A pup splashed water.
8. The pup jumped out.
9. Joe ran after the pup.
10. The pup made tracks.
11. The children laughed.

Sample Answers 1. Predicate 6. Joe | gave his pups a bath.

Subject Parts and Predicate Parts

You have learned about the two parts of a telling sentence. Every telling sentence has a subject part and a predicate part. The *subject part* names whom or what the sentence is about. The *predicate part* tells what action the subject part does.

Each part alone is not a sentence. It does not state a complete idea. You make a sentence when you join the subject part and the predicate part.

● Look at the subject parts and predicate parts below. Choose a subject part and a predicate part. Join the parts to make a sentence. Make as many sentences as you can using these parts.

SUBJECT PARTS	PREDICATE PARTS
The gray squirrel	dug a hole.
His friends	looked for nuts.
The squirrels	found many nuts.

Talk About It

Make a sentence using each of these subject parts. What part do you need to add?

1. The children ____ .
2. The little turtle ____ .

Make a sentence using each of these predicate parts. What part do you need to add?

3. ____ rode a horse.
4. ____ climbed a tree.

Skills Practice

Join each subject part with a predicate part. Write the sentences you have made.

1. The birds
2. The children
3. Jay and Bonita
4. Other children
5. The happy birds
6. Two dogs
7. Three cats
8. The sisters

paint in red.
feed them.
ride bicycles.
sing a song.
build a house for them.
live in the tree.
run around the tree.
sit in the sun.

Writing Sentences

Add a predicate part or a subject part to complete each sentence. Write the sentences.

1. Leslie ____ .
2. The girls ____ .
3. An owl ____ .
4. ____ drank milk.
5. ____ went to sleep.
6. ____ watched us play.

Read each sentence. Look at the part in the box.
Write **subject** if it is a subject part. Write **predicate**
if it is a predicate part.

1. Kay | planted a garden.
2. The neighbors | helped.
3. The neighbors | planted corn.
4. Kay | saw that birds like corn.
5. A scarecrow | scared the birds.
6. The corn plants | grew very tall.
7. Kay | picked the corn.
8. The neighbors | cooked some corn.
9. Kay | had a picnic.
10. The neighbors | brought ice cream.

Write each sentence. Draw a line between the
subject part and the predicate part.

11. Barry had a pet dragon.
12. The dragon liked blueberry pancakes.
13. Barry picked some blueberries.
14. The pet dragon made the pancakes.
15. The friends ate the pancakes.

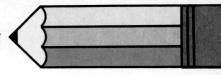

Make some sentences. Join each subject part with a predicate part. Write the sentences you have made.

16. Pam   walked to the store.
17. Her sister   saved her money.
18. The girls   bought a present.
19. The family   opened the present.
20. Mother   sang a song.

Think of a subject part or a predicate part to complete each sentence. Write each sentence.

21. The boy ___ .
22. A pony ___ .
23. My friends ___ .

24. ___ moved the chair.
25. ___ saw a rocket.
26. ___ rolled away.

Write each word on a card or a piece of paper.

KITTEN   A   TINY   YESTERDAY   RICK   FOUND   .

Put the words in order to make a sentence. Make as many different sentences as you can. Be sure your sentences make sense.

Exploring Language

Parts of a Book

Most school books have more than one part. It is easier to use a book when you know how to use the parts.

The *table of contents* is at the front of the book. It shows what is in the book. It lists the number and name of each unit or chapter. It also tells on what page each unit or chapter begins. You can use the table of contents to learn about the book.

The *index* is at the back of the book. It lists all the things the book tells about. It is in alphabetical order. The index helps you find things quickly.

Sometimes a book may have special parts before the index. Look at the back of this book. A special part called the Handbook begins on page 286. You can use the *handbook* to find important rules about your language.

Talk About It _____

Use this book to answer these questions.

1. How many units are in this book?
2. On what page does the first page of Unit 3 begin?
3. What is the name of the first lesson in Unit 4?
4. On what page does the index begin?
5. What is listed first in the index?
6. What is listed first in the handbook?

Skills Practice _____

Use the table of contents on page 18 to answer these questions. Write the answers.

1. What is the book about?
2. What is the name of Chapter 5?
3. Which chapter begins on page 15?
4. Is there a chapter about rabbits?
5. On what page does the index begin?

Use the index on page 18 to answer these questions. Write the answers.

6. What pages tell about sharks?
7. What pages tell about turtles?
8. What page tells about salmon?

Learning About Paragraphs

You know how to write a sentence. A sentence is a group of words that states a complete idea.

Sometimes it takes more than one sentence to tell or explain something. Then you need to use a group of sentences.

A **paragraph** is a group of sentences that tells about one main idea.

The sentences in a paragraph must work together. The first sentence in a paragraph often states the most important idea of the paragraph. This sentence is called the *main idea sentence*. The other sentences tell more about the main idea. They are called *detail sentences*.

A **main idea sentence** states the most important idea of the paragraph.

Detail sentences tell more about the main idea.

- Read this paragraph about Donna and her cat. What is the main idea sentence? What are the detail sentences?

Donna takes good care of her cat.
First she feeds the cat.
Next she plays with the cat.
Then she brushes the cat.

Did you find the main idea sentence in the paragraph about Donna? Did you find the details? Here is a way to see how they work together.

Main idea: Donna takes good care of her cat.
Detail 1: First she feeds the cat.
Detail 2: Next she plays with the cat.
Detail 3: Then she brushes the cat.

Talk About It

Read this paragraph. What is the main idea sentence? What are the detail sentences?

Two robins raised a family in our tree. First the mother robin laid four eggs in a nest. Then she sat on them. Now the robins have four noisy babies.

Skills Practice

Write these labels on your paper.

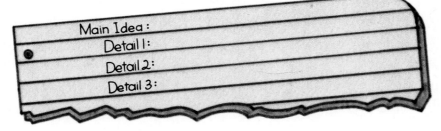

Main Idea:
Detail 1:
Detail 2:
Detail 3:

Read this paragraph. Fill in the main idea and details on your paper.

Our class raised some frogs. First we got some frog eggs. Then the eggs grew into tadpoles. At last the tadpoles became baby frogs.

Time Order in Paragraphs

Thinking About Paragraphs

You know that the words in a sentence must be in an order that makes sense. The sentences in a paragraph must also be in an order that makes sense.

Here is one good way to arrange the sentences in a paragraph.

1. Start with a main idea sentence. This sentence tells what the paragraph will be about.

2. Add detail sentences to tell more about the main idea. Put your detail sentences in *time order*. Tell what happened *first*. Tell what happened *next*. Tell what happened *last*.

● Read this paragraph about Mr. Paso.

Mr. Paso works in a pet shop. First he opens the store. Next he feeds the pets. Then he cleans their cages. Last he lets us play with the pets.

The first sentence tells the main idea of the paragraph. It tells about Mr. Paso's job in a pet shop. The detail sentences are in time order. They tell what he does first, next, and last. They are in an order that makes sense.

Look at the first word in the paragraph about Mr. Paso's job. It is moved in a little space from the left margin. It is *indented*. Indenting helps the reader know where a new paragraph begins. Indent the first word of a paragraph.

Talking About Paragraphs

Read these detail sentences. They are not in time order. Put them in a time order that makes sense.

1. a. Later the chipmunk ran home with the nut.
  b. First the chipmunk looked around carefully.
  c. Next the chipmunk picked up the big nut.

Read these sentences. They tell about one idea. Choose the main idea sentence. Then put the detail sentences in a time order that makes sense.

2. a. First Kevin slipped on the ice.
  b. Next Father took him to the doctor.
  c. Kevin broke his arm.
  d. Now Kevin wears a cast on his broken arm.

Writing a Paragraph

Read these sentences. They tell about one idea. Choose the main idea sentence. Then put the detail sentences in a time order that makes sense. Write the paragraph. Remember to indent the first word.

  a. Last she put the pots in a sunny window.
  b. Jane started a window garden.
  c. Then she watered the seeds.
  d. First she filled some pots with dirt and seeds.

A Class Paragraph

Thinking About Paragraphs

Your class is going to write a paragraph together. The pictures will help you. They show how Bert fixed a bed for his new puppy. The pictures are in the right time order to make sense.

Writing a Paragraph

1. Your paragraph will start with a main idea sentence. The main idea sentence is *Bert made a bed for his new puppy.* Your teacher will write it on the board.

2. Think of a detail sentence that tells about the first picture. Your teacher will write it on the board.

3. Think of detail sentences for the next two pictures. Your teacher will write them.

4. Copy the paragraph on your paper. Remember to indent the first word.

Your Own Paragraph

Thinking About Your Paragraph

Now you are going to write your own paragraph. The pictures will help you. They show how George built a birdhouse.

The Word Bank will help you, too. It shows how to spell some of the words you may want to use.

Writing Your Paragraph

1. Your paragraph should start with a main idea sentence. The main idea sentence is *George built a birdhouse*. Write this sentence on your paper. Remember to indent the first word.

2. Look at the first picture. Write a detail sentence that tells about the picture. Use your Word Bank to help you spell your words.

3. Write a detail sentence about the next picture.

4. Now write a detail sentence about the last picture.

5. Save your paragraph.

Word Bank

first
next
then
last
boards
father
hammer
nail
paint
green

How to Edit Your Work

After you write a paragraph, it is a good idea to edit it. *Edit* means to read carefully and fix any mistakes.

Look at the paragraph you wrote about George's birdhouse.

First be sure your paragraph says what you want it to say. Check for these things:

1. Look at your main idea sentence. Does it tell what all the pictures are about?

2. Are your detail sentences in a time order that makes sense?

3. Does each sentence state a complete idea?

4. Do the words in the sentences come in an order that makes sense?

Next be sure other people can read your paragraph. Check for these things:

5. Did you indent the first word?

6. Did you start each sentence with a capital letter and end it with a period?

7. Did you spell all the words correctly? Remember to use your Word Bank.

Read Jane's paragraph. What mistakes did Jane make? How did she correct them?

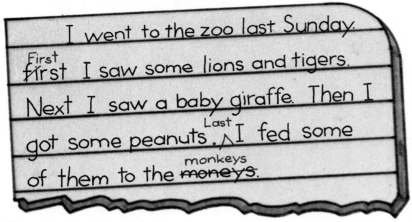

I went to the zoo last Sunday.
First
first I saw some lions and tigers.
Next I saw a baby giraffe. Then I
                         Last
got some peanuts.ʌI fed some
                    monkeys
of them to the ~~moneys~~.

Edit Your Paragraph

Edit your paragraph about George's birdhouse. Use the seven check questions. Correct all your mistakes. You may want to make a good copy of your paragraph to share with the class.

Careers

A doctor who takes care of animals is called a *veterinarian.* Veterinarians work with animals. They help to keep animals well. Veterinarians go to school for many years. They must read about all the things that make animals sick. Veterinarians also must write directions for taking care of animals. Would you like to be a veterinarian? You can start by learning to read and write very well.

Robert Houser

Checking Skills

Read the groups of words in each pair. Write each group of words that is a sentence. *pages 2–3*

1. The horse eats hay.
The horse.

2. A cow.
A cow gives milk.

3. Some pigs roll in the mud.
Some pigs.

4. The chickens lay eggs.
The chickens.

Read each sentence. Write **telling** if it is a telling sentence. Write **question** if it is a question sentence. Write **exclamation** if it is an exclamation sentence. *pages 6–7*

5. Did you go to the zoo?
6. Did you see the bears?
7. A seal swam in a pool.
8. Two monkeys hung by their tails.
9. What a funny monkey that is!

Some special signs are missing in each sentence. Write each sentence correctly. *pages 8-9*

10. our class has a turtle.
11. Who feeds the turtle
12. how slowly the turtle eats
13. Cathy brought a snake to school
14. we keep the snake in a box

Checking Skills

Read each sentence. Look at the part in the box.
Write **subject** if it is a subject part. Write **predicate**
if it is a predicate part. *pages 12–15*

15. Three bears | lived in the woods.

16. The bears | went for a walk.

17. A girl | found their house.

18. The girl | went inside.

19. The girl | found a bed.

20. The girl | fell asleep.

21. The bears | came home.

22. The bears | found the girl.

23. The girl | ran home.

Read these detail sentences. They are not in time
order. Write them in a time order that makes sense. *pages 22–23*

24. **a.** Next we painted the house bright green.
    b. Last we put food inside for the birds.
    c. First we built a bird house out of wood.

Read these sentences. Choose the main idea
sentence. Then put the detail sentences in a time
order that makes sense. Write the paragraph. *pages 22–23*

25. **a.** Then the family drove to the picnic area.
    b. First they made the food for the picnic.
    c. Ming's family went on a picnic on Sunday.
    d. Last everyone sat on the ground and ate.

Reading a Story

Do you have a favorite place to play by yourself? It may be one corner of a park or a little part of your house. It may be a secret place that no one else knows about.

In this story a boy takes you to his secret places. They are in the woods near his house. He tells about his secret places in order. First he talks about some people who used to live in the woods. Then he talks about the woods today. Last he tells about something new in the woods.

You may find some new words in this story. The words and their meanings are listed under *Words to Think About*. Look at *Words to Think About*. Then read the story.

Words to Think About

settlers, people who make a home in a new place

olden days, a long time ago

meadow, a field of grass

Secret Places

I have a secret place in the woods I call
Old Log Cabin. Settlers built it in the
olden days. They lived here, they ate
here, and at night they slept here. There
aren't any more settlers, but there were.
Now there are only woods, lots of woods.

I have a secret place in the woods I call
The Fishing Hole. Frogs hop by it, water
splashes into it, and fish swim in it. There
aren't many fish, there are only some.
But there are woods, lots of woods.

I have a secret place I call The Meadow. Grasshoppers hop here, flowers grow here, crickets chirp here, and birds sing here, in the woods, in all the woods.

I have a secret place in the woods I call The Forest. I dance here, I climb here, I run here, and I play here. The woods are the prettiest place I know. And there are woods, lots of woods.

I know another place in the woods. It has no name. Diggers dig there, trucks drive there, houses grow there, and people work there. I hope they never find my secret places.

D. J. Arneson

Activities _____

1. **Creative Writing** Imagine a secret place that only you know about. Write a paragraph that tells what your secret place looks like, or write a paragraph that tells what you like to do there.

2. Think about your secret places. Draw pictures of some of them. Show what you like to do in each place. Put the pictures in the order that you like to visit the places.

3. Pretend you are a bug with a secret place in your classroom. Tell how to get from your secret place to the door of the room. See if your classmates can guess the secret place.

Grammar and Related Language Skills

Nouns
Singular and Plural Nouns
Common and Proper Nouns
Names, Addresses, and Dates

Practical Communication

Using a Dictionary
Writing a Descriptive Paragraph

Creative Expression

Poetry

Learning About Nouns

You know that a sentence states a complete idea. Now you will learn about words that help state ideas in sentences.

> A **noun** is a word that names a person, a place, or a thing.

Kate and Eric took a bus trip last summer. The picture shows some people, places, and things that they saw.

- Name some *people* Kate and Eric saw. Name the *place* shown in the picture. Name some *things* that Kate and Eric saw. The people, places, and things that you named are all nouns. What other people, places, and things do you think Kate and Eric saw on their trip?

- Read each of these sentences. Why is the word in the box a noun?

I took a bus to $\boxed{\text{Topeka}}$. The $\boxed{\text{bus}}$ traveled very fast.

My $\boxed{\text{mother}}$ went, too. I saw many $\boxed{\text{buildings}}$.

Talk About It _____

Read each sentence. Then read the nouns.

1. Meg got in the car.
2. A woman rode on the bus.
3. The streets were very bumpy in Centertown.
4. The girl visited her grandmother.

Skills Practice _____

Read each sentence. Write the nouns.

1. Mike flew in an airplane.
2. A girl sat nearby.
3. Her friend wore glasses.
4. A man waved from the ground.
5. A strong wind blew in his face.
6. The boy landed in St. Louis.

Writing Sentences _____

Pretend you visited a big city. Tell what you saw.

1. Write a sentence with a noun that names a person.
2. Write a sentence with a noun that names a place.
3. Write a sentence with a noun that names a thing.

Sample Answer 1. Mike airplane

Nouns in Sentences

You use nouns almost every time you make sentences. Some nouns are in the subject part of a sentence. To find nouns in the subject part, remember these two things.

A **noun** is a word that names a person, a place, or a thing.

The **subject part** of a sentence names whom or what the sentence is about.

- Look at the subject part of each sentence. Read each noun.

The **gate** closed in front of us.

A long **train** raced by.

The **engineer** blew the whistle.

Sometimes nouns are in the predicate part of a sentence. Remember,

The **predicate part** of a sentence tells what action the subject part does.

- Look at the predicate part of each sentence. Is there a noun in the predicate part? What is it?

Rosalie rode on a **train** .

The engine chugged .

The train went to **Chicago** .

Talk About It

Read these sentences. What are the nouns in the subject parts? What are the nouns in the predicate parts?

1. Many people hurried through the station.
2. A boy carried two bags.
3. Nadia got on the train.

Skills Practice

Write each sentence. Draw a line under each noun.

1. The children rode on the train.
2. Henry ran to the first car.
3. Isabel sat next to a window.
4. The whistle blew.
5. Cows watched the train pass.
6. Pete ate apples for lunch.
7. Rick visited the engine.

Writing Sentences

Pretend you are riding a train. Think of a noun for each blank. Write each sentence.

1. Our trip took us to ___ .
2. A ___ took a picture of the train.
3. The ___ made noise all night.
4. ___ wrote letters to ___ .

Sample Answer 1. The children rode on the train.

Singular and Plural Nouns

Some nouns name only one person, place, or thing. Other nouns name more than one person, place, or thing.

A **singular noun** is a noun that names one person, place, or thing.

pirate   sea   ship

A **plural noun** is a noun that names more than one person, place, or thing.

pirates   seas   ships

Singular and plural nouns have different forms. The form shows if the noun names one or more than one.

- Look at the forms of the nouns in each box. Which nouns are singular? Which nouns are plural?

| car | driver | town |
| cars | drivers | towns |

The plural nouns in the boxes end with *s*.

- Look at the picture below. Which card belongs under each picture? Why?

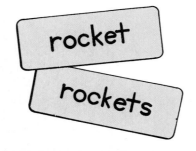

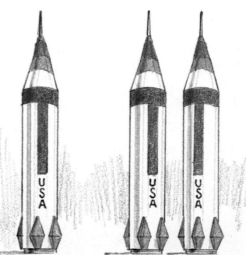

Talk About It

Choose the noun that belongs in the blank in each sentence. Tell if it is singular or plural.

1. Three ___ rode on their bikes. (boy, boys)
2. One ___ got a flat tire. (bike, bikes)
3. Another bike hit many ___. (rock, rocks)
4. This bike has two flat ___. (tire, tires)
5. They could not ride on one ___. (bike, bikes)
6. The three ___ returned home. (boy, boys)

Skills Practice

Write each noun. Then write **singular** if the noun is singular. Write **plural** if the noun is plural.

1. dog
2. kittens
3. chairs
4. table
5. pond
6. aunts
7. uncle
8. cups
9. duck

Write each sentence with the correct noun.

10. Karen went for a ___. (walk, walks)
11. Many of her ___ joined her. (friend, friends)
12. All the ___ met at the park. (girl, girls)
13. They hiked for two ___. (mile, miles)
14. Sara lost a ___ along the way. (shoe, shoes)
15. It fell near a ___. (stream, streams)
16. The girls looked for ten ___. (minute, minutes)
17. A ___ found the shoe. (friend, friends)

Sample Answers 1. dog, singular 10. Karen went for a walk.

Forming Plural Nouns

Singular nouns name one person, place, or thing. Plural nouns name more than one person, place, or thing. You can make a singular noun into a plural noun by changing the form of the word.

> To make most singular nouns plural, add an **s**.

• Read each pair of nouns. Does each noun name one or more than one? Is each noun singular or plural? What was added to each singular noun to make it plural?

truck	bridge	garage	mountain
truck**s**	bridge**s**	garage**s**	mountain**s**

Sometimes you have to add *es* to make a singular noun plural.

> If a singular noun ends with **s, ss, x, ch,** or **sh,** add **es** to write the plural.

• Read each pair of nouns. Does each noun name one or more than one? Is each noun singular or plural? What was added to each singular noun to make the plural form?

bus	dress	box	branch	dish
bus**es**	dress**es**	box**es**	branch**es**	dish**es**

Sometimes you have to change the spelling of a noun before you add *es* to make it plural.

If a singular noun ends with a **consonant** and **y**, change the **y** to **i** and add **es** to write the plural.

baby ⟶ babies
babi + es

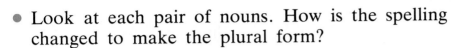

• Look at each pair of nouns. How is the spelling changed to make the plural form?

country   city   penny
countries   cities   pennies

Talk About It

Spell the plural of each noun.

1. party	**4.** family	**7.** puppy	**10.** baby
2. tree	**5.** dress	**8.** clock	**11.** dish
3. fox	**6.** shirt	**9.** ranch	**12.** class

Skills Practice

Write the plural of each noun.

1. bunny	**4.** window	**7.** car	**10.** country
2. blueberry	**5.** door	**8.** cherry	**11.** crow
3. bus	**6.** city	**9.** wish	**12.** fly

Writing Sentences

Read the words below. Write four sentences. In each sentence, use the plural of one of these words.

pony   splash   toy   story

Sample Answer 1. bunnies

More Plural Nouns

You already know how to write the plural of most nouns. Some singular nouns form the plural in a different way. You have to learn the plural of these nouns.

- Look at each noun below.

tooth	⟶ teeth	child	⟶	children
ox	⟶ oxen	goose	⟶	geese
man	⟶ men	mouse	⟶	mice
foot	⟶ feet	woman	⟶	women

Talk About It

Read each sentence. At the end of each sentence is a singular noun. Say the plural of the noun.

1. Two ___ swam in the pond.   (goose)
2. All three ___ are doctors.   (woman)
3. Both of José's ___ hurt.   (foot)
4. A team of ___ pulled the cart.   (ox)

Skills Practice

Write the plural of these nouns.

1. man	5. foot
2. goose	6. ox
3. tooth	7. child
4. woman	8. mouse

Sample Answer 1. men

Making New Words

You can make new words from some words you already know. One way of making new words is to add *er* to the end of certain words. Each new word tells what kind of work a person does.

- Look at each pair of words.

climb
climb**er**

print
print**er**

Someone who <u>climbs</u> is a <u>climber</u>.

Someone who <u>prints</u> is a <u>printer</u>.

Talk About It

Look at the underlined word. Change it into a word to tell what kind of work the person does. Your answer should make sense in the blank.

1. Mr. Caplan <u>teaches</u> school.
Mr. Caplan is a ___ .

2. Ms. Janson <u>drives</u> a bus.
Ms. Janson is a bus ___ .

Skills Practice

Look at the underlined word in each pair of sentences. Change it into a word to tell what kind of work the person does. Write the sentence.

1. Bob <u>plays</u> baseball.
Bob is a baseball ___ .

3. Mrs. Kato <u>reports</u> the news.
Mrs. Kato is a news ___ .

2. Ellen <u>writes</u> stories.
Ellen is a ___ .

4. Mr. Como <u>builds</u> houses.
Mr. Como is a ___ .

Sample Answer 1. Bob is a baseball player.

Skills Review

Read each sentence. Write the nouns.

1. The children borrow books from the library.
2. The woman walked quickly.
3. Mr. Johnson drove the children to school.
4. Carlos ran along the road.
5. The dogs played with the ball.
6. My mother works in a bank.
7. The boys raced home.

Write each sentence. Draw a line under each noun.

8. Ms. Clark picked the apples.
9. A robin landed on the ground.
10. Joey watched the game.
11. The car honked.
12. The bus stopped by the tree.
13. The babies drank the milk.
14. Many people enjoy the park.

Write each noun. Then write **singular** if the noun is singular. Write **plural** if the noun is plural.

15. pitcher	18. cat	21. streets	24. shoe
16. brooks	19. wishes	22. ranch	25. foxes
17. day	20. river	23. frogs	26. pennies

Write the correct noun for each sentence.

27. Some children visited a ____ . (park, parks)
28. Five ____ played on the swings. (girl, girls)

29. Three ____ hunted for bugs.   (boy, boys)

30. The boys caught two ____ .   (fly, flies)

31. The children ate lunch under a ____ .   (tree, trees)

32. Two ____ drove through the park.   (bus, buses)

33. Sally found a ____ on the ground.   (dollar, dollars)

34. She put the money in a ____ .   (pocket, pockets)

Write the plural of each noun.

35. wagon	**39.** story	**43.** dish
36. room	**40.** city	**44.** ox
37. toy	**41.** rabbit	**45.** foot
38. glass	**42.** family	**46.** mouse

Look at the underlined word. Change it into a
word that tells what kind of work the person does.
Write the new word.

47. Amy <u>trains</u> animals.
Amy is an animal ____ .

48. Roy <u>farms</u> the land.
Roy is a ____ .

49. Leroy <u>skates</u> on ice.
Leroy is an ice ____ .

50. Betty <u>climbs</u> mountains.
Betty is a mountain ____ .

Make as many nouns as
you can. You can use only
the letters in this noun:

astronaut

Exploring
Language

Proper and Common Nouns

You know that a noun names a person, place, or thing. Some nouns name special people, places, and things.

A **common noun** is a noun that names any person, place, or thing.

A **proper noun** is a noun that names a special person, place, or thing.

May has five turtles. Here are their names.

Rocky   King   Snappy   Bowser   Snoop

When May says the word *turtle,* she could be talking about any turtle. The word *turtle* is a common noun. When she says the word *Snappy,* you know she is talking about a special turtle. *Snappy* is a proper noun.

● Read each pair of nouns. Which is a common noun? Which is a proper noun?

Susan	boy	Hill School
girl	Paul Ramos	school
city	Alaska	statue
San Francisco	state	Statue of Liberty

Many proper nouns have more than one word.

Begin each important word in a proper noun with a capital letter.

• Look again at the proper nouns in the box. Which words begin with capital letters?

Talk About It

Look at the nouns that are underlined. Tell whether each noun is a proper noun or a common noun.

1. A <u>woman</u> climbed <u>Mount Ap</u>.
2. <u>Snow</u> covered the <u>mountain</u>.
3. The <u>top</u> was in the <u>clouds</u>.
4. A <u>man</u> wrote about her <u>trip</u>.

Harvey Lloyd, Peter Arnold Photo Archives

Skills Practice

1. Find the proper nouns in the box. Write them.
2. Find the common nouns in the box. Write them.

baseball	Empire State Building	Johnny Appleseed
mountain	apple	city
Dayton	Toronto Blue Jays	Rocky Mountains

Write each noun. Write **proper** if it is a proper noun. Write **common** if it is a common noun.

3. The boy lives near Forest Park.
4. Carlos Rivera skates at the park.
5. Myra rides her bike.
6. The children from Webster School visit in April.
7. Many people have picnics in the park.
8. Jean walks home on Elm Street.

Sample Answer 3. boy, common, Forest Park, proper

Writing Proper Nouns

All people have names. Their names are proper nouns. There is a special way to write proper nouns that name people.

- Look at the picture. What are the names of the children? Are the names proper nouns?

Sometimes people use initials instead of their full names.

An **initial** is the first letter of a name.
Write an initial with a capital letter.
Put a period after the letter.

- Look at these ways of writing the same name. How are initials used in each one?

Thomas Adam Cantor   Thomas A. Cantor
T. A. Cantor   T. A. C.

- Look at the picture. How would you use initials to write the names of the children?

Some people use titles in front of their names.

Begin a **title** with a capital letter.
End most titles with a period.

• Read the titles in these names. Which of these titles does not end with a period?

Dr. Lisa Jones   Mrs. Ann Ramirez   Ms. Leslie Zhan

Mr. Albert Penson   Miss Jane Costa

Talk About It

How would you write each of these names?

1. mrs robertson
2. miss masters
3. mr mark m jensen
4. dr carla boone

Skills Practice

Write each name correctly.

1. mrs d silver
2. mr cramer
3. linda l stevens
4. dr michael koval

Write each sentence correctly.

5. Did tommy ryan tell you?
6. Our class gave mr walker a party.
7. We invited dr anders to come.
8. I helped sandy rosen make lemonade.
9. P j carlin read a story by laura ingalls wilder.

Writing Sentences

Write two sentences about yourself.

1. Use your full name in a sentence.
2. Use your initials in a sentence.

Sample Answers 1. Mrs. D. Silver 5. Did Tommy Ryan tell you?

Writing Addresses and Dates

You know that proper nouns can name special people. Each name begins with a capital letter. Now you will learn how to write names of special places and days.

Use **capital letters** to begin proper nouns that name places.

● Find the proper nouns in this picture. What do they name?

The names of streets begin with capital letters.

Spring Street   Elm Road

The names of cities and states begin with capital letters.

Greenburg   Ohio

Put a **comma** (,) between the name of the city and the state when you write them together.

Greenburg, Ohio

Sometimes you need to show where someone lives.

An **address** shows where someone lives.

An address shows the house number, the name of the street, the city, the state, and the ZIP code. It is often written with a person's name. Each proper noun in an address begins with a capital letter.

Sometimes you need to write the date. You use a comma between the day of the month and the year.

> Use a **comma** (,) to separate the day of the month from the year.

April 7, 1981   October 30, 1982

Talk About It

How should each of these names and dates be written?

1. oak street
2. orangetown
3. mill avenue

4. gary indiana
5. weston vermont
6. dallas texas

7. June 4 1983
8. August 22 1981
9. May 13 1981

Skills Practice

Write each name and address correctly.

1. dr jan mills
   36 adams street
   chicago illinois 60607

2. mr sam henson
   615 rabbit road
   sun city arizona 85351

Write each date correctly.

3. April 10 1982
4. August 13 1980
5. February 6 1981

6. October 8 1983
7. January 30 1982
8. December 23 1984

Write each noun. Write **proper** if it is a proper noun. Write **common** if it is a common noun.

1. The woman helped build Peachtree Center.
2. Joe Turner works at the station.
3. The boy goes to Lakeland School.
4. The children visited the San Diego Zoo.
5. A girl saw the squirrel.
6. The man drove along Ocean Avenue.
7. Bob Walker got into the car.

Write each sentence correctly. Make sure you write each name correctly.

8. Gail goldberg went to the library.
9. Mr teller read stories by r l jones.
10. Then ms b a kaywood sang a song.
11. Dr j k martin helped mrs anita lind with the food.
12. We visited miss rose w carter.

Write each name and address correctly.

13.
> don ito
> 47 mountain avenue
> denver colorado 80220

14.
> mr manuel gomez
> 54 orange road
> somerset kentucky 42501

15.

> ms dora williams
> 21 main street
> redkey indiana 47373

16.

> dr kim wu
> 2 forest road
> fargo north dakota 58102

Write each date correctly.

17. January 1 1936

18. May 30 1922

19. March 8 1963

20. October 24 1975

21. December 30 1976

22. November 6 1981

In early times, people were known by the kind of work they did. In a small town, there might be a few men named Jack. To make clear which person they were talking about, they would say *Jack the Miller* or *Jack the Miner*. In time, they became Jack Miller and Jack Miner. Think of some other names that might have come about in the same way.

Exploring Language

Dictionary: Alphabetical Order

When you read, you may find words that are new to you. You may want to learn how to spell words. You can find out more about words by using a dictionary.

All the words in a dictionary are written in alphabetical order. *Alphabetical order* means that words are placed in the same order as the letters of the alphabet. You must know how to use alphabetical order to use the dictionary.

A B C D E F G H I J K L M N O P Q R S T U V W X Y Z

Here is a list of words. Look at the first letter of each word. These letters come in the same order as the letters of the alphabet. So these words are in alphabetical order.

> fox
> man
> ring

● Look at the three words in each list. Are they in alphabetical order?

ask	door	win
boy	play	toy
car	zoo	song

Here is another list of words. All these words begin with the same letter. Look at the second letter of each word. These letters come in the same order as the letters of the alphabet. So these words are in alphabetical order.

> clock
> come
> cut

- Look at the three words in each list. Are they in alphabetical order?

four	dance	milk	seeds
fish	deer	money	salt
from	drum	mule	soup

Talk About It

Put each list of three words in alphabetical order.

1. free	**2.** question	**3.** noise
desk	invite	name
hammer	garage	news

Skills Practice

Write each list of three words in alphabetical order.

1. cap	**4.** some	**7.** under
ant	splash	up
bat	score	use
2. block	**5.** apple	**8.** giant
beside	over	school
bird	down	goat
3. cold	**6.** mark	**9.** eleven
huge	dragon	engine
hear	snow	east

Sample Answer 1. ant
bat
cap

Using a Dictionary

The words in a dictionary are in alphabetical order. This means that the words come in the same order as the letters of the alphabet.

You may want to know if a list of words is in alphabetical order. Look at the first letter of each word. The letters should come in the same order as the letters of the alphabet. Many words begin with the same letter. Then you must look at the second letter. These two lists are in alphabetical order.

detective	**w**elcome
helicopter	**wh**ale
trail	**wo**rker

Suppose the first and second letters of each word are the same. Then you must look at the third letter to see if the words are in alphabetical order.

● Look at the three words in each list. Are they in alphabetical order?

be**g**inning	**g**rant	**mi**rror
be**a**n	g**r**in	**mi**stake
be**l**ow	g**ro**cery	**mi**x

You can find words in a dictionary more quickly if you know which part to turn to. Think of dividing the dictionary into two parts. All words beginning with *a* through *m* are in the first part. All words beginning with *n* through *z* are in the second part.

- Read each word. Would you find it in the first part or the second part of a dictionary?

vegetable   company   practice   horn

Talk About It

Put each list of three words in alphabetical order.

1. drop	**2.** themselves	**3.** beach	**4.** state
written	ticket	bend	storm
march	television	bee	steam

Skills Practice

Write each list of three words in alphabetical order.

1. frog	**2.** open	**3.** teacher	**4.** problem
could	many	talk	prepare
train	minute	thin	print

Read each word at the left. Does it come between the words in **a** or in **b**? Write the letter of the correct pair of words.

5. lesson **a.** lend, let   **6.** friend **a.** four, frame
            b. letter, life   **b.** fresh, frog

Would you find each word in the first part or the second part of a dictionary? Write your answer.

7. language   **8.** polite   **9.** sky   **10.** edge

Sample Answers 1. could frog train 5. a 7. first part

Paragraphs That Describe

Thinking About Paragraphs

You can write paragraphs to tell about different things. One kind of paragraph tells what something is like. This kind of paragraph can tell how something looks. It can tell how something tastes or feels. It may even tell how something smells or sounds. This kind of paragraph describes something or someone.

• Read this paragraph. It describes a puppet.

> My puppet looks like Snow White. She has brown buttons for eyes. Her hair is made from black wool. She wears a dress made from red cloth. Her dress feels very soft.

Talking About Paragraphs

1. What is the main idea sentence in the paragraph?

2. Which detail sentences tell what the puppet looks like?

3. Which detail sentence tells what the dress feels like?

4. How do you think the puppet sounds?

5. Now you have read about the puppet. Can you draw a picture of the puppet?

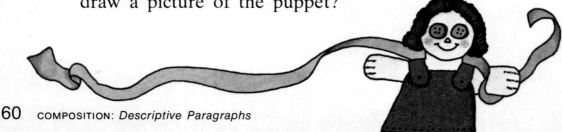

Writing a Class Paragraph

Now you can write a paragraph with your class. Look at the picture below. It shows how Bobby dressed on Halloween. Write a paragraph to describe how he dressed. Your teacher will write all your sentences on the board.

1. The main idea sentence is *Bobby wore a pirate costume on Halloween.* Your teacher will write it on the board.

2. Look at the picture of Bobby's costume. Think of a detail sentence to describe his hat. Your teacher will write it on the board.

3. Think of a detail sentence to describe his coat.

4. Now look at his face. Think of a detail sentence to describe it.

5. Read your paragraph. Does it describe how Bobby dressed?

6. Copy the paragraph on your paper. Be sure to indent the first word.

Your Own Paragraph

Thinking About Your Paragraph

Now you can write your own paragraph. Pretend you got a new puppy. Write a paragraph describing your new puppy. You may want to use some of the words in the Word Bank.

Word Bank

black
white
brown
floppy
tail
paws
coat
soft
small

Writing Your Paragraph

1. Write this main idea sentence on your paper. *I have a new puppy named Lucky.* Remember to indent the first word.

2. Write a detail sentence to tell how big Lucky is. Use the Word Bank to help you spell your words.

3. Write a detail sentence to tell what color Lucky is.

4. Write a detail sentence to describe his ears.

5. Write another detail sentence to tell about Lucky.

Edit Your Paragraph

Read your paragraph again. Does your paragraph say what you want it to say?

1. Does each detail sentence describe your new puppy?

2. What nouns did you use?

3. Is each noun a singular noun or a plural noun?

Be sure other people can read your paragraph.

4. Did you indent the first word?

5. Did you begin and end each sentence correctly?

6. Did you begin each proper noun with a capital letter?

7. Did you spell all the words correctly?

Fix your mistakes. Make a good copy of your paragraph to share with your class.

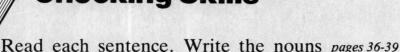

Checking Skills

Read each sentence. Write the nouns *pages 36-39*

1. The girl rows a boat.
2. Two boys fish from the dock.
3. Many people sail on the big ship.
4. A woman waves from the deck.

Write each sentence with the correct noun. *pages 40-41*

5. My friend pulled a red ___ . (wagon, wagons)
6. Two ___ rode in it. (kitten, kittens)
7. They slept in a straw ___ . (basket, baskets)
8. Three ___ saw the kittens. (girl, girls)
9. My brother wanted a ___ . (kitten, kittens)

Write the plural of each noun. *pages 42-44*

10. dress	12. country	14. foot
11. jet	13. bench	15. fox

Change the underlined word in each pair of sentences to tell what kind of work the person does. *page 45*

16. Mr. Black <u>teaches</u> school.
    Mr. Black is a ___ .

17. Rose <u>hikes</u> in the woods.
    Rose is a ___ .

18. You <u>play</u> hockey.
    You are a hockey ___ .

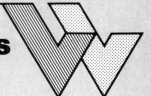

Write each noun. Write **proper** if it is a proper noun.
Write **common** if it is a common noun.   *pages 48-49*

19. The children went to Florida.
20. Robin liked Disney World.
21. Simon swam at Miami Beach.
22. Dr. Ross took the train to New York.
23. The train stopped at Baltimore.

Write each name and address correctly.   *pages 50-53*

24. ms isabel minsky
35 west end avenue
new york new york 10011

25. mr alonso pérez
18 green street
baker nevada 89311

Write each date correctly.   *pages 52-53*

26. May 15 1926
27. June 6 1984
28. March 12 1982

29. June 3 1963
30. January 10 1983
31. February 12 1982

You are going to write a paragraph that describes a
cat. Here is the main idea sentence: *Our new cat is
beautiful.* Here are words you may use in your
detail sentences.   *pages 60-63*

white	gray	yellow	glow	dark	tiny

32. Write the main idea sentence of the paragraph.
33. Write a sentence that describes the cat's hair.
34. Write a sentence that describes the cat's eyes.
35. Write a sentence that describes the cat's feet.

Poetry

A *poem* is a special way to paint pictures in words. When you read a poem, you can see pictures in your mind. The writer chooses each word carefully. The meaning of each word must fit the idea in the poem. These poems are about ways to travel. Your teacher will read each poem to you. Try to picture what the words describe.

BUS RIDE

I hailed the bus and I went for a ride
And I rode on top and not inside
As I'd done on every other day:

The air was so sweet and the city so gay
The sun was so hot and the air so mellow

And the shops were bursting with green and yellow.

The shops were the brightest I'd ever seen—
Full of yellow and pink and green,
Yellow in this and green in that,
A dress or a kerchief, a tie or a hat,

And I wanted to dance and I wanted to sing
And I bought a flower because it was spring.

Selma Robinson

Song of the Train

(*softly*)
Clickety-clack,
Wheels on the track,
This is the way
They begin the attack:

(*louder*)
Click-ety-clack,
Click-ety-clack.
Click-ety, *clack-ety,*
Click-ety,
Clack.

(*louder*)
Clickety-clack,
Over the crack,
Faster and faster
The song of the track:
Clickety-clack,
Clickety-clack,
Clickety, clackety,
Clackety,
Clack.

(*softly*)
Riding in front,
Riding in back,
Everyone hears
The song of the track:
Clickety-clack,
Clickety-clack,
Clickety, *clickety,*
Clackety,
Clack.

—*David McCord*

Activities

1. In "Bus Ride" find words for colors and things to wear that add to the picture of spring. In "Song of the Train," what words sound like train noises?

2. **Creative Writing**   Think of interesting words to go in the blanks. Write the sentences. The first one is done for you.

   Lightning is like <u>a crack in the sky</u>.
   Sunshine is like_____.
   Thunder is like _____.

Grammar and Related Language Skills

Verbs
Verbs in the Present
Verbs in the Past
Spelling Verbs

Practical Communication

Using Test-Taking Skills
Following and Giving Directions
Writing a Direction Paragraph
Writing an Invitation

Creative Expression

A Picture Story

Learning About Verbs

You do many things each day. Sometimes you want to tell someone about the things you do. Then you need to use words that name actions. Words like *skip* and *hop* name actions.

- Look at the picture.

  What action is the girl doing with the rope?
  What action is the boy doing with the ball?
  What action is the dog waiting to do?

  > A **verb** is a word that names an action.

- Read each sentence. What action does each verb name?

  Mark <u>hops</u> on one foot.   Paco <u>tosses</u> a ball.
  Jean <u>jumps</u> rope very fast.   His dog <u>catches</u> the ball.

Talk About It

Read each sentence. Is each underlined word a verb?

1. Maria <u>walks</u> to the park after school.
2. The boy <u>rides</u> his skateboard.
3. <u>Sharon</u> skips down the street.
4. A girl <u>pulls</u> a red wagon.
5. A <u>dog</u> chases a squirrel.

Skills Practice

If the underlined word is a verb, write **verb.** If the underlined word is not a verb, write **not verb.**

1. Ken <u>throws</u> the ball.
2. <u>Dora</u> swings the bat.
3. A girl <u>hits</u> the ball hard.
4. Jim <u>catches</u> the ball.
5. Jim throws the <u>ball</u> to Carlos.
6. Carlos <u>drops</u> the ball.
7. Dora <u>runs</u> to second base.

Writing Sentences

Think of a verb for each blank. Write each sentence.

1. My brother ____ his bicycle.
2. Rita ____ to the playground.
3. Mei ____ the football.
4. A cat ____ over the fence.

Sample Answer 1. verb

Verbs in Sentences

Verbs are important in sentences. You can find verbs in the predicate parts of sentences. Remember these two facts.

A **verb** is a word that names an action.

The **predicate part** of a sentence tells what action the subject part does.

● Look at the predicate part of each sentence. Read each verb.

Ben **walks** on the beach.
The man **runs** into the water.
Jan **dives.**
The woman **splashes** some water.

The main word in the predicate part of a sentence is the verb. The verb names the *action* that the subject part does.

● Read each sentence. Find the verb. What action does it name? The picture can help you.

My friends swim in a pool.
Ray splashes water on Sue.
Joe dives into the pool.
Maria floats on her back.

Talk About It

Read each sentence. Find the verb.

1. Our family drives to the lake every Sunday.
2. My cousins swim all day.
3. The babies build sand castles.
4. My mother puts a blanket on the sand.
5. Kim opens the picnic basket.
6. Her father swims in the deep water.

Skills Practice

Write each sentence. Underline the verb.

1. The class hikes in the woods.
2. The teacher carries a pack on his back.
3. The students pitch a tent.
4. Akiko builds a fire.
5. José cooks the food.
6. The teacher tells ghost stories.
7. Anna climbs into her sleeping bag.
8. An owl hoots.

Writing Sentences

Pretend you are having a picnic. Write four sentences to tell what you do on a picnic. Use these verbs.

1. run
2. throw
3. eat
4. sing

Sample Answer 1. The class hikes in the woods.

Verbs in the Present

A verb names an action. A verb can also tell *when* the action happens. Sometimes you talk about things that happen now.

- Look at these sentences that tell about the picture.

The girl <u>rides</u> a big horse.
The horses <u>jump</u> over the fence.

The sentences tell about things that happen now.
The verbs *rides* and *jump* are verbs in the present.

A **verb in the present** names an action that happens now.

- Read each sentence.

John <u>walks</u> to the barn.   John <u>walked</u> to the barn.
Andy <u>cleans</u> the stall.   Andy <u>cleaned</u> the stall.
Paula <u>saddles</u> her horse.   Paula <u>saddled</u> her horse.

Look at the verbs in the sentences at the left. These verbs are verbs in the present. Look at the verbs in the sentences at the right. They are not in the present.

Talk About It _____

Find the verb in each sentence. Is the verb in the present?

1. Jane runs to the stable.
2. A little colt stands in a stall.
3. Jane hugs the colt.
4. The colt eats a piece of carrot.
5. The horses kicked their legs.
6. Jane talked to the colt.
7. The horses trot out of the stable.

Skills Practice _____

Read each sentence. Write **present** if the verb is in the present. Write **not present** if the verb is not in the present.

1. My sisters ride horses in the parade.
2. My dad tied ribbons on the horses.
3. Two other horses pull a wagon.
4. A family waits in the wagon.
5. Some children wave flags.
6. My mom waved to the children.
7. A man sells candy.
8. The band marches.
9. The band played my favorite song.
10. The crowd cheers loudly.
11. A police officer rides a horse.
12. The horse trots to the music.

Sample Answer 1. present

Using Verbs in the Present

You know that nouns are often in the subject parts of sentences. Remember that the *subject part* of a sentence names whom or what the sentence is about. Nouns in the subject part can be singular or plural.

A **singular noun** is a noun that names one person, place, or thing.

A **plural noun** is a noun that names more than one person, place, or thing.

● Read each sentence. Look at the noun in the subject part. Then look at the verb.

The boy run**s**.　　　Two boys run.

The sentences show that the verb must work with the noun in the subject part. The verb has different forms to work with singular and plural nouns.

● Read each pair of sentences. What is the ending on each verb? How does each verb change to work with the noun in the subject part?

Kurt *plays* with a ball.　　The boys *play* marbles.
Kate *makes* candles.　　　Her sisters *make* paper airplanes.

Most verbs in the present end in *s* when they work with a *singular* noun. Most verbs in the present do not change at all when they work with a *plural* noun.

Talk About It

Read each sentence. Choose the verb that works with the noun in the subject part.

1. Carmen ___ paper flowers. (make, makes)
2. Her sisters ___ colored paper. (buy, buys)
3. Sara ___ the paper into pieces. (cut, cuts)
4. Paul ___ the pieces together. (paste, pastes)
5. The boys ___ the edges. (fold, folds)

Skills Practice

Write each sentence. Use the correct verb.

1. The boys ___ a lump of clay. (find, finds)
2. Brian ___ a big piece. (take, takes)
3. Fred ___ his clay. (mold, molds)
4. The boy ___ a little house. (build, builds)
5. Two girls ___ their clay. (shape, shapes)
6. Their clay ___ into a vase. (turn, turns)
7. Mother ___ more clay. (buy, buys)

Writing Sentences

Pretend you and some friends are home on a rainy day. You have crayons, paper, and scissors. You are each going to make something.

1. Write one sentence to tell about what *one* friend makes.
2. Write one sentence to tell what *two* friends make together.

Sample Answer 1. The boys find a lump of clay.

Spelling Verbs

A verb in the present has different forms. You must know how to spell the form of the verb that you use in a sentence.

● Read each sentence.

The girl skates.   Kim paints.

The noun in each subject part is singular. The verb that works with each noun ends in *s*.

> Add **s** to most verbs in the present when they work with singular nouns.

Sometimes you add *es* to a verb in the present when it works with a singular noun.

● Now read these sentences.

A player passes the football.   Nancy watches the game.

Notice the singular noun in each subject part. Each verb ends in *es*.

> If a verb ends in **s, ss, ch, sh,** or **x,** add **es** to make the verb work with a singular noun.

Sometimes you change the spelling of a verb before you add *es*.

● Read each sentence. Notice that the spelling changes when this verb works with a singular noun.

The birds fly.   A bird flies.

If a verb ends with a **consonant** and
y, change the **y** to **i** and add **es** to
make the correct form of the present.

Verbs in the present that work with *plural* nouns do
not change.

● Read each sentence below.

Two boys sing a song.   The students listen.

Notice the nouns in the subject part. They are
plural nouns. The verbs do not change.

Talk About It

What form of the verb belongs in each blank? Spell
the verb.

1. Roberto ____ games. (like)
2. A little boy ____ a kite. (fly)
3. Tara ____ him. (watch)

Skills Practice

Use a verb in the present in each blank. Write the
sentence.

1. The students ____ hide-and-seek. (play)
2. Liza ____ behind a tree. (hide)
3. Gino ____ to find her. (try)
4. The girl ____ out. (peek)
5. The boy ____ her. (catch)

Sample Answer 1. The students play hide-and-seek.

If the underlined word is a verb, write **verb.** If the underlined word is not a verb, write **not verb.**

1. Molly <u>finds</u> a pretty leaf.
2. Rita <u>traces</u> it on paper.
3. The girl writes with a <u>pencil</u>.
4. A <u>boy</u> colors it.
5. Peter <u>cuts</u> it out.
6. The teacher <u>pins</u> it to the board.

Read each sentence. Write the verb.

7. The boys make a book cover.
8. Jerry buys some brown paper.
9. Pablo cuts a piece of it.
10. Ben folds the piece in half.
11. Carl puts the book on it.
12. The girls bend the edges around the book.

Read each sentence. Write **present** if the verb is in the present. Write **not present** if the verb is not in the present.

13. Matt finds a shell at the beach.
14. The shell sparkled in the sun.
15. Carol makes a necklace.
16. Her father cleaned the shell.
17. Her mother drilled a hole in it.
18. Carol puts a ribbon through the hole.
19. Carol likes the necklace.

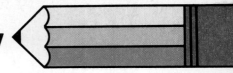

Read each sentence. Write the correct verb.

20. Anna ___ a garden.   (plant, plants)
21. Her father ___ some holes.   (dig, digs)
22. Mike ___ the seeds.   (buy, buys)
23. The girls ___ the garden.   (water, waters)
24. The seeds ___ .   (grow, grows)

Use a verb in the present in each blank. Write the verb.

25. Judy ___ in the shade.   (sit)
26. Her sister ___ the ducks in the pond.   (watch)
27. Judy ___ a swan.   (see)
28. The boys ___ around.   (run)
29. Ducks ___ fish.   (like)
30. The bird ___ away.   (fly)
31. My father ___ the children.   (call)
32. A dog ___ the pond.   (pass)

Play this verb game. Have one person write five different verbs (such as, *dance, hop, throw*) on five pieces of paper. Fold the papers and put them in a hat.

Someone chooses a paper and acts out the verb. The class tries to name the action being done. The person who guesses the answer must spell the verb. He or she then becomes the next person to act out a verb.

Exploring Language

Verbs in the Past

Some verbs name actions that happen now. Other verbs name actions that happened before.

The boy climbs a tree.　　　　The boy climbed a tree.

- Look at the sentence under each picture. The sentence on the left tells about something that happens *now*. The sentence on the right tells about something that happened *before*. *Climbed* is a verb in the past.

  > A **verb in the past** names an action that happened before.

- Read each sentence. What is the verb? Is the verb in the past?

  Adam <u>played</u> in the treehouse.　Jean <u>opened</u> the door.
  A girl <u>knocked.</u>　　　　　　　　Lucy <u>chases</u> a squirrel.

  Look at the underlined words. They are verbs. The first three verbs are in the past. They tell what happened before. The last verb is in the present.

Talk About It

Find the verb in each sentence. Is the verb in the past?

1. The children played with model trains.
2. The train moves on the track.
3. Ann pulled the engine.
4. The train crossed the bridge.
5. Jack pushed the train.
6. The children listen to the whistle.

Skills Practice

Read each sentence. Write **past** if the verb is in the past. Write **not past** if the verb is not in the past.

1. Mandy raced home.
2. The girl called her brother.
3. Jim plays games.
4. Mandy played cards.
5. Her brother opened a drawer.
6. Jim hands a deck of cards to Mandy.
7. Mandy counted the cards.
8. Mandy changes the score.
9. The children played all afternoon.
10. The children like the game.
11. Mandy wins very often.
12. Jim added the scores.
13. The boy continued the game.
14. Their mother called them.
15. The children started their homework.

Sample Answer 1. past

Spelling Verbs in the Past

Sometimes you talk about something that happened before. You use a verb in the past. Most verbs in the past have the same ending.

Add **ed** to most verbs to make a verb in the past.

If a verb ends with **e**, drop the **e** and add **ed** to make the correct form of the past.

- Read each sentence. Look at the verb.

The family camped in the forest.   Ed cooked.
Paula moved the tent.   A wolf howled.

The verbs are in the past. Each verb ends in *ed*.

Sometimes you have to change the spelling of a verb before you add *ed*.

- Look at each pair of verbs.

tr**y**	carr**y**	cop**y**
tr**ied**	carr**ied**	cop**ied**

You can see that the spelling changes for each verb in the past.

If a verb ends with a **consonant** and **y**, change the **y** to **i** and add **ed** to make a verb in the past.

Talk About It

Find the verb in each sentence. Is it about the past or the present? How can you tell?

1. The friends hiked for a long time.
2. Inés finds a good place for a camp.
3. Debra fished in the lake.
4. Barry fried fish over the fire.

Skills Practice

Write each sentence. Use the verb in the past.

1. Amy ___ the trail last week.   (mark)
2. The boys ___ the packs then.   (carry)
3. Ed ___ many interesting leaves yesterday.   (pick)
4. The girls ___ the dishes after lunch.   (dry)
5. Larry ___ the dishes to the tent.   (move)
6. Ed ___ the new flashlight.   (try)
7. The family ___ the dinner last night.   (like)
8. The friends ___ the trip last week.   (enjoy)

Writing Sentences

Pretend you slept in a tent in the woods last night. Write two sentences about something that happened.

Sample Answer 1. Amy marked the trail last week.

Verbs That Are Alike

You and your friends do not always use the same words to tell about the same thing. Sometimes you use different verbs to tell about the same thing in different ways.

- Read each sentence about the picture.

The children *walked*. The children *hiked*.
The children *marched*. The children *strolled*.

The sentences tell about the same thing. The verbs *walked, marched, hiked,* and *strolled* all mean almost the same thing. But the verb *marched* most closely names the action in the picture.

You can write better sentences if you choose verbs carefully. The verb you choose can change the meaning of a sentence.

- Read each sentence. How does each verb change the sentence?

The boy ___ the package. (carried, hauled)
A girl ___ to school. (ran, raced)

Talk About It _____

Read each sentence about the picture. Which verb most closely names the action in the picture?

1. The horse ___ in the park.
   (walks, trots)
2. Linda ___ the reins.
   (holds, has)
3. The horse ___ the wagon.
   (pulls, moves)
4. Steve ___ to Linda.
   (speaks, whispers)

Skills Practice _____

Read each sentence about the picture. Choose the verb that most closely names the action in the picture. Write the sentence.

1. Ray ___ the batter.
   (stirs, makes)
2. Ray ___ on a stool.
   (sits, perches)
3. Ray ___ a cup of flour.
   (takes, grabs)
4. Ray ___ the spoon.
   (has, holds)
5. Ray ___ the bread.
   (bakes, cooks)
6. Ray ___ the bread.
   (cuts, breaks)

Sample Answer 1. Ray stirs the batter

Skills Review

Read each sentence. Write **past** if the verb is in the past. Write **not past** if the verb is not in the past.

1. Linda walks in the woods.
2. Robin picked some flowers.
3. Betty walked with her friends.
4. A deer jumped over a log.
5. The girls play under a tree.
6. Mark dried the twigs.
7. Linda feeds a squirrel.
8. The girl carried the rock.
9. The children chased a butterfly.
10. Linda searched for a bird's nest.

Read each sentence. Write the verb in the past.

11. Diana ___ baseball. (play)
12. The girl ___ the ball to Jack. (toss)
13. The boy ___ on first base. (jump)
14. Our mother ___ the children. (call)
15. My grandmother ___ dinner. (cook)
16. Jack ___ Diana home. (follow)
17. Bill ___ his dog yesterday. (walk)
18. The dog ___ a cat. (chase)
19. The cat ___ a tree. (climb)
20. The dog ___ a new dog food. (try)
21. Bill ___ to his dog. (wave)
22. Bill ___ home. (hurry)

Read each sentence about the picture. Choose the verb that most closely names the action in the picture. Write the verb.

23. Dennis ___ on the ground.
    (moved, crawled)
24. The boy ___ a bird's nest.
    (saw, studied)
25. Marie ___ a heavy basket.
    (dragged, carried)
26. The girl ___ hello to Dennis.
    (said, shouted)
27. A duck ___ to the lake.
    (waddled, walked)

Look at the sentence.

    I *walked* to school.

Try to think of other verbs you can use instead of *walked* that mean almost the same thing. Go around the room and ask each person in your class to put a different verb in the sentence. Those who cannot think of one must drop out. The winner is the last person left who knows another word for *walked*.

Exploring
Language

Following and Giving Directions

Sometimes you have to tell someone how to do something. *Directions* tell you how to do things. You must follow directions carefully to do things in the right way.

Ben's teacher gave the class two directions. First she asked them to draw a picture of what they like best in the park. Next she asked them to write a sentence about their pictures.

● Look at the children's papers.

Lee followed directions. His picture shows what he likes best in the park. His sentence tells what he likes best in the park. Rob's picture shows something in the park. But he did not write a sentence. Cindy's picture just shows something she likes. It is not about the park.

Directions can tell how to get somewhere. Good directions make sense. They help people to find places easily. Be sure you tell things in the right order when you give directions.

Maps can help you give directions.

- Find Lee's house on the map. Follow these directions to get to the park from Lee's house.

First walk up Pine Road to School Street.
Next turn left at School Street.
Last walk to the park.

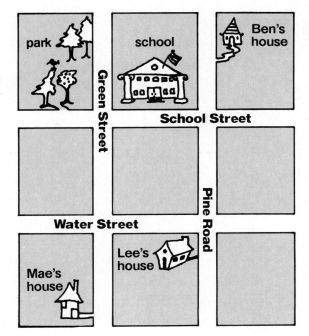

Talk About It

Use the map above. Give directions to get from Mae's house to school. Use words like *first, next,* and *last* in your directions.

Skills Practice

Mae gave directions to get from her house to Ben's house. Her directions are not in the right order. Write them in the correct order. Use the map above to help you. Use words like *first, next,* and *last* when you write the directions in order.

Turn right at Water Street and walk to Pine Road.
Walk up Green Street to Water Street.
Turn left at Pine Road and walk up to Ben's house.

Using Test-Taking Skills

You take many tests in school. Tests can help you find out what you know. They can also help you find out what you need to study some more. You can help yourself do better on tests if you follow a few rules.

1. **Get Ready.** Be sure that you have pens, pencils, and paper for taking the test.
2. **Follow Directions.** Listen carefully if your teacher reads the directions to you. Read the directions carefully if you read them to yourself.
   Be sure to ask any questions before you begin.
3. **Mark your answers.** Be sure you mark your answers in the correct place. Often you write your answers beside the questions on your test paper. Sometimes you write your answer under the questions. Other times you use a separate answer sheet.

- Look at the test below. In this example, answers are marked in a special place on the test paper.

Choose the right word to complete each sentence. Fill in the circle for the right answer. Write only in the answer row.	Name _Sue Jones_ Date _May 8, 1981_ Grade _3-C_ Answer Row
1. The plural of train is ___. **A.** traine **B.** trains **C.** train	**1.** A B C ○ ● ○
2. The plural of bus is ___. **A.** busse **B.** buss **C.** buses	**2.** A B C ○ ○ ●

Talk About It

Look again at the test paper.

1. Find where you would write your name.
2. What two things would you write below your name?
3. How would you mark the right answer to the first question? The second?

Skills Practice

Read the following test paper. Look carefully at how the person has followed directions. Write the answers to the questions below on your own paper.

Choose the right word to complete each sentence. Fill in the circle for the right answer. Write only in the answer row.	Name *Luis Vargas* Date *3-A* Grade *March 6, 1981* Answer Row
1. The girls *find* pretty rocks. **A.** finds **B.** find	**1.** A B ○ ○
2. Father ____ a long walk. **A.** takes **B.** take	**2.** Ⓐ B ○ ○
3. The boys *play* a new game. **A.** play **B.** plays	**3.** A B ● ○

1. What is wrong with the date and the grade?
2. How should the right answer to the first question be marked?
3. What is wrong with how the answer to the second question is marked?
4. What is wrong with how the answer to the third question is marked?

Direction Paragraphs

Thinking About Paragraphs

Directions are important. They tell people the things they need to know. Directions must always be clear. Then people understand what to do.

Pretend you are standing at a busy street corner. The traffic light is broken. Cars do not know when to go and stop. People do not know when to cross the street. Someone has to give them directions.

At times you may have to give directions. Sometimes you can write them down. You can write your directions in a paragraph. The paragraph has a main idea sentence and several detail sentences. The main idea sentence tells what the directions are for. The detail sentences tell how to do or make something. Each detail sentence gives one step of the directions. The sentences must come in an order that makes sense. They should tell what to do first, second, and third.

● Read this paragraph that gives directions. Find the main idea sentence and the detail sentences.

It is fun to make a fruit basket. First you find a large basket. Second you put in an apple, a pear, and an orange. Third you tie a ribbon around the basket.

The first sentence gives the main idea. The detail sentences give the steps in an order that makes sense. The words *first, second,* and *third* tell the order of the steps.

The first word in the paragraph is indented. This shows that a new paragraph is beginning.

Talking About Paragraphs

Read these sentences. Choose the main idea sentence. Then put the detail sentences in the right order.

a. Third you let yourself down slowly.
b. Second you pull yourself up to your chin.
c. A chin-up is easy to do.
d. First you hang by your hands from a bar.

Writing a Paragraph

Todd wrote these directions to get from his house to the library. They are not in the right order. Use the map to help you. Write the directions in the correct order. You may use the words *first, second,* and *third* if you wish.

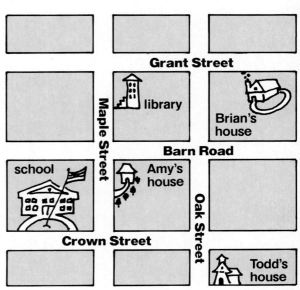

Turn right and walk to the library.
Walk up Oak Street to Barn Road.
Turn left and walk to Maple Street.

A Class Paragraph

Thinking About Paragraphs

Your class is going to write a paragraph together that gives directions. The pictures will help you. They show how to brush your teeth. The pictures are in the right order to make sense.

Writing a Paragraph

1. Your paragraph will start with a main idea sentence. The main idea sentence is *Brushing your teeth is easy.* Your teacher will write it on the board.

2. Think of a detail sentence that tells what to do in the first picture. Your teacher will write it.

3. Think of detail sentences for the next two pictures. Your teacher will write them.

4. Copy the paragraph on your paper. Remember to indent the first word.

Your Own Paragraph

Thinking About Your Paragraph

You are going to write your own paragraph about how to make a bean bag. You may also choose your own topic.

Writing Your Paragraph

1. Start your paragraph with this main idea sentence: *A bean bag is fun to make.*

2. Look at the pictures. Write detail sentences that give directions for making a bean bag. You will have three detail sentences.

3. Use the Word Bank to help you spell the words.

Edit Your Paragraph

Read your finished paragraph. Think about these questions as you read.

1. Can you make a bean bag by following your directions?

2. What verbs did you use in your detail sentences? Does each sentence have a verb that tells what to do?

Word Bank

cut
cloth
beans
middle
fold
sew
thread

3. Are capital letters and periods used correctly? Did you indent the first word?

4. Did you spell all words correctly? Correct your mistakes. Make a good copy of your paragraph.

Invitations

Thinking About Invitations

Pretend you are planning a party. Notes must be sent to the people you want to invite. These notes are called *invitations*. An invitation tells people what they need to know about the party.

- Look at the invitation below.

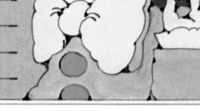

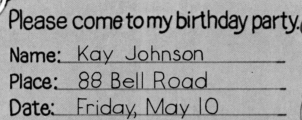

Please come to my birthday party.
Name: Kay Johnson
Place: 88 Bell Road
Date: Friday, May 10
Time: 4:00
Telephone: 588-9842

Talking About Invitations

Read the invitation above.
1. Who is giving the party?
2. Where and when is the party being held?
3. What telephone number can people call to say if they are coming?

Writing an Invitation

Write your own invitation. Copy the part of the above invitation that is in dark print. Then write your own name. Write the place, date, and time of the party. Give your telephone number so people can call you.

Telephone Messages

Thinking About Telephone Messages

Sometimes you take directions instead of giving them. For example, you might answer a telephone call that is for someone else. You need to take a message that tells about the call.

- Look at the telephone message below.

A call for: Jill
Caller's name: David Murphy
Time: 1:00
Message: David is coming to your party.
Caller's number: 566-3209
Message taken by: Burt

Talking About Telephone Messages

1. Who was the above message for? Who called?
2. What time was the call? What was the message?
3. What is the caller's number? Who took the message?

Writing a Telephone Message

Pretend you have a brother named Jim who is planning a birthday party. At 4:30 Martha Keller calls Jim to say she cannot come to the party. Martha's phone number is 533-5892. Copy the part of the above message that is in dark print. Then fill in the information.

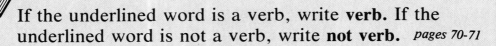

Checking Skills

If the underlined word is a verb, write **verb.** If the underlined word is not a verb, write **not verb.** *pages 70-71*

1. Mario <u>walks</u> in the rain.
2. <u>Diane</u> steps in a puddle.
3. The girl <u>wears</u> boots.
4. A boy carries a <u>coat</u>.

Read each sentence. Write the verb. *pages 72-73*

5. Jim builds a snow fort.
6. The boys skate here.
7. Judy throws a snowball.
8. Carol rides her sled.

Read each sentence. Write **present** if the verb is in the present. Write **not present** if the verb is not in the present. *pages 74-75*

9. Cindy enjoys the breeze.
10. A baby laughed happily.
11. The boy wears a sweater.
12. Dave jumps down.

Read each sentence. Write the correct verb. *pages 76-77*

13. The boy ____ a big kite. (make, makes)
14. The wind ____ hard. (blow, blows)
15. The kite ____ on the breeze. (sail, sails)
16. Our friends ____ the kite. (follow, follows)

Use a verb in the present in each blank. Write the verb. *pages 78-79*

17. Karen ____ a piece of paper. (fold)
18. Her little brother ____ her. (watch)
19. The boy ____ the paper airplane. (fly)
20. Some girls ____ more toys. (make)

Read each sentence. Write **past** if the verb is in the past. Write **not past** if the verb is not in the past. *pages 82-83*

21. The children played hockey.
22. Joe skated very fast.
23. Maria hits the puck.
24. Their team scored a goal.

Read each sentence. Write the verb in the past. *pages 84-85*

25. Stan ____ the eggs.   (cook)
26. The girls ____ the bread.   (butter)
27. Ruth ____ the potatoes.   (fry)
28. The family ____ the breakfast.   (like)

Now you will write an invitation.

29. Here is the information you include in an invitation. Write it on your paper. *page 98*

Name: _____

Place: _____

Date: _____

Time: _____

Telephone: _____

Pretend that John Williams is planning his birthday party. It is to be held at 25 Oak Lane on June 24. The party will start at 2:00. John's phone number is 589-5332. Write the invitation that John will send to his friends.

A Story in Pictures

Most stories are told in words. Some stories can be told without using any words. A story can be told in pictures. Each picture tells part of the story. You must study each picture to understand what happens in the story.

Look at each picture in this story.

CREATIVE EXPRESSION: *Non-verbal Communication*

CREATIVE EXPRESSION: *Non-verbal Communication*

Activities

1. **Creative Writing** The children in *The Surprise* made a *piñata*. Do you think they were surprised by what was hidden inside? Write a paragraph that tells how to make a *piñata*. Use the pictures to help you.

2. Pretend you are one of these people. Act out what the person is doing. Do not speak. Ask the class to guess what you are doing.

   A person climbing many stairs
   A batter hitting a ball
   A person flying a kite
   A lion tamer with a lion

3. Make pictures of your own. Think about what you want in each picture. How will your story begin and end? How many pictures will your story have? Share your picture story with someone.

Grammar and Related Language Skills

Practical Communication

Creative Expression

Three Kinds of Sentences

You have learned about three kinds of sentences.

A **telling sentence** is a sentence that tells something.

A **question sentence** is a sentence that asks something.

An **exclamation sentence** is a sentence that shows strong feeling.

● Read each sentence. Is it a telling sentence, a question sentence, or an exclamation sentence?

What a funny puppet show we saw!
Did you ever see a talking potato?
A boy put a potato on a stick.
He painted a face on the potato.
How funny the jokes were!
Do you like puppet shows?

You use special signs when you write sentences. One special sign shows where each sentence begins. You use other special signs to show where a sentence ends.

Use a **capital letter** to begin the first word of every sentence.

Use a **period** (.) at the end of a telling sentence.

Use a **question mark** (?) at the end of a question sentence.

Use an **exclamation mark** (!) at the end of an exclamation sentence.

Talk About It

Read each sentence. Look at the beginning and end of each sentence. What special signs are missing?

1. The class saw a puppet
2. Who moved the puppet
3. How hard we laughed
4. a puppet told a story.
5. can puppets really talk
6. Can we make puppets

Skills Practice

Write each sentence correctly. Then write **telling** if it is a telling sentence. Write **question** if it is a question sentence. Write **exclamation** if it is an exclamation sentence.

1. Juan likes to sing
2. he listens to the radio.
3. did you hear a new song
4. do you like music?
5. can you play the piano?
6. how well Karen plays!
7. she likes to sing, too.
8. what a pretty song that is!

Sample Answer 1. Juan likes to sing. Telling

Complete Sentences

You have learned that a sentence is a group of words that states a complete idea. Every sentence has a subject part and a predicate part.

> The **subject part** of a sentence names whom or what the sentence is about.

> The **predicate part** of a sentence tells what action the subject part does.

Each part alone is not a sentence. The two parts work together to state a complete idea.

SUBJECT PART	PREDICATE PART
The cook	made blueberry pancakes.

● Read each group of words. Which groups of words are sentences?

The baker makes bread.　　Eats the bread.
The baker.　　　　　　　Barbara eats the bread.

● Read each sentence. Find the subject part. Find the predicate part.

A scientist found some old bones.
People put the bones together.
The people make a dinosaur.

Talk About It

Read each group of words. Is it a complete sentence? What do you need to add to make a complete sentence?

1. A ball player.
2. The team wins a game.
3. Hits a home run.
4. Sells orange juice.
5. The team.
6. The crowd yells.

Skills Practice

Write each sentence. Draw a line between the subject part and the predicate part.

1. A train moves fast.
2. The man buys a ticket.
3. People go many places.
4. The bell rang.
5. The class stands up.
6. A girl opens the door.

Add a subject part or a predicate part to complete each sentence.

7. The teacher ____ .
8. My doctor ____ .
9. A bus driver ____ .
10. ____ sells shoes.
11. ____ draws pictures.
12. ____ throws a ball.

Writing Sentences

Pretend you are a TV star. Write a telling sentence about being a TV star. Be sure your sentence has a subject part and a predicate part.

Sample Answer 1. A train | moves fast.

Nouns and Verbs in Sentences

You know that words like *Chris, street,* and *apple* name people, places, or things.

> A **noun** is a word that names a person, a place, or a thing.

Most sentences have a noun in the subject part. Some sentences have a noun in the predicate part.

- Read each sentence. Find the noun in the subject part. Is there a noun in the predicate part?

The show starts.   The crowd likes the show.
A dancer jumps in the air. The dancer bows.

You know that words like *run* and *jump* name actions.

> A **verb** is a word that names an action.

Every sentence has a verb in the predicate part.

- Read each sentence. Find the verb.

Patty brought some wood. Snappy likes the doghouse.
Len painted the doghouse. Snappy sleeps on the roof.

Remember that the verb must work with the noun in the subject part.

- Read each pair of sentences. How does the verb change to work with the noun in the subject part?

The teacher <u>helps</u>. One cook <u>makes</u> lunch.
The teachers <u>help</u>. Two cooks <u>make</u> soup.

Talk About It

Read these sentences. Find the nouns and verbs.

1. The builders make houses.
2. The workers build a roof.
3. A man paints the walls.
4. The boy opens a window.
5. A woman fixes the doors.
6. A girl hangs pictures.

Skills Practice

Write each sentence. Draw one line under each noun. Draw two lines under each verb.

1. A girl plants seeds.
2. The little plants grow.
3. Plants grow in the sun.
4. Horses eat hay.
5. The flowers bloom.
6. A girl works on a ranch.
7. The man rides a horse.
8. The horses live in a barn.
9. A girl waters the plants.
10. A horse trots.

Write the correct verb for each sentence.

11. My friend ___ on a farm. (live, lives)
12. The chickens ___ corn. (eat, eats)
13. A goat ___ the flowers. (like, likes)
14. The farmers ___ very hard. (work, works)
15. The pigs ___ in the pen. (sit, sits)
16. A horse ___ in the field. (run, runs)

Writing Sentences

Pretend that you drive a bus. Write two sentences about two different things you might do on your job. What nouns and verbs did you use?

Sample Answers 1. A girl plants seeds. 11. lives

Skills Review

Write each sentence correctly. Then write **telling** if it is a telling sentence. Write **question** if it is a question sentence. Write **exclamation** if it is an exclamation sentence.

1. how badly my arm hurts!
2. did you fall?
3. you should go to the doctor
4. What happens there
5. the doctor looks at your arm.
6. what a big machine he uses!
7. the doctor can see you now.

Read each sentence. Write the subject part.

8. The pilot flies a big airplane.
9. The airplane travels very fast.
10. An airplane flew to Detroit.
11. Many people ride on airplanes.
12. Animals fly on airplanes.

Read each sentence. Write the predicate part.

13. People eat on airplanes.
14. Airplanes fly over the ocean.
15. My suitcase fell off the plane.
16. A man found the suitcase.
17. A woman gave the suitcase to me.

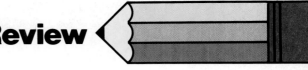

Read each sentence. Write the nouns.

18. The woman plows the field.
19. Andy plants corn.
20. The farmers feed the chickens.
21. The chickens eat.
22. The chickens gobble the corn.

Read each sentence. Write the verbs.

23. Robin sews shirts.
24. Joy works in a store.
25. The store buys the shirts.
26. Many people look at the shirts.
27. Joy sells the new clothes.

Write the correct verb for each sentence.

28. A child ____ a book. (read, reads)
29. A man ____ the house. (clean, cleans)
30. The dancers ____ pretty clothes. (wear, wears)
31. The cooks ____ soup. (make, makes)
32. The woman ____ . (write, writes)

Find three nouns in a newspaper. Cut them out. Draw a picture to show what each noun names.

Exploring Language

Pronouns in Sentences

Many sentences have nouns in the subject part. Sometimes you can use other words in place of these nouns.

A **pronoun** is a word that takes the place of one or more nouns.

These are the pronouns that can be used in the subject part of a sentence.

I	you	she he it
we		they

Remember to use a capital letter for the pronoun *I*.

- Read each pair of sentences. What pronoun is in the subject part of the second sentence in each pair? What noun does each pronoun replace?

Rita makes a basket.
She makes a basket.

The girls make kites.
They   make kites.

Eddie paints two bowls.
He   paints two bowls.

The market opens early.
It   opens early.

- Read these sentences. What is the pronoun in each sentence?

I paint the room.
You fix the chair.
We work hard all day.

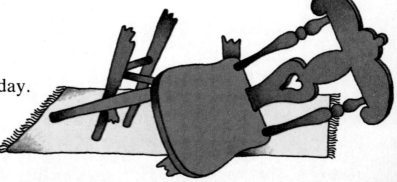

Talk About It

Read each pair of sentences. Write the second sentence using the correct pronoun.

1. <u>Ben</u> works in the city.
   ____ sells cars.

2. <u>Jenny</u> works in the city.
   ____ writes books.

3. <u>Jenny and Ben</u> ride.
   ____ ride a train.

4. <u>The train</u> leaves early.
   ____ is crowded.

Skills Practice

Write each sentence. Underline each pronoun.

1. I shoveled snow.
2. You helped.
3. We earned a dollar.
4. They watched.

Read each pair of sentences. Write the second sentence using the correct pronoun.

5. <u>Mrs. Lee</u> drives a bus.
   ____ drives carefully.

6. <u>The bus</u> goes to school.
   ____ is full of children.

7. <u>Ed</u> rides the bus.
   ____ sits quietly.

8. <u>Ed and Jane</u> sit together.
   ____ sing together.

9. Mr. Harris is a teacher.
   ____ teaches third grade.

10. The bell rings.
    ____ rings again.

11. Jane raises her hand.
    ____ answers the question.

12. Jane and Ed carry books.
    ____ have homework today.

Sample Answers 1. <u>I</u> shoveled snow. **5.** She drives carefully.

Using Pronouns and Verbs

The subject part of every sentence has a noun or a pronoun. The predicate part has a verb. You know that nouns and verbs must work together in a sentence. Pronouns and verbs must also work together in a sentence.

- Read each sentence. Name each pronoun. What ending is used on each verb?

He teach**es** ice skating.
She pick**s** fruit.
It fall**s** off trees.

- Read these sentences. What pronouns are used? Verbs used with these pronouns do not have *s* or *es* endings.

Pam Hasagawa

You skate very well.
They pack the fruit in boxes.
We like the fruit.
I eat fruit before skating.

- Read each sentence. Find the pronoun and verb. Do they work together in each sentence?

I enjoy ice skating.
She enjoys skating.
We skate together every week.
He skates very fast.

Talk About It

Use the correct verb in each sentence.

1. He ___ a truck every day. (drive, drives)
2. I ___ my homework quickly. (finish, finishes)
3. They ___ cars. (fix, fixes)
4. She ___ in a post office. (work, works)

Skills Practice

Use the correct verb in each sentence. Write the verb.

1. We ___ in the snow. (play, plays)
2. I ___ the snow fall. (watch, watches)
3. They ___ the schools. (close, closes)
4. We ___ home when it snows. (stay, stays)
5. They ___ the roads in the afternoon. (plow, plows)
6. You ___ cold quickly. (get, gets)
7. He ___ the walk. (shovel, shovels)
8. She ___ a heavy coat all winter. (wear, wears)
9. It ___ her warm. (keep, keeps)
10. We ___ to school today. (return, returns)

Writing Sentences

Pretend you work in a pet store. Write a sentence using each pronoun. Be sure to use the correct verb.

1. I   **2.** it   **3.** they   **4.** we

Sample Answer 1. play

Possessive Pronouns

You know that a pronoun is a word that takes the place of one or more nouns. *Possessive pronouns* show who or what has or owns something.

A **possessive pronoun** is a pronoun that shows who or what has or owns something.

- Suppose your name were Tom. You want to talk about your brother. If you could not use possessive pronouns, you would have to say:

Tom's brother works in a store.

- Now read this sentence.

<u>My</u> brother works in a store.

This time, the possessive pronoun *my* is used in place of the possessive noun *Tom's*.

- Look at the box. The possessive pronouns on the left are used in sentences on the right.

my	<u>My</u> mother owns a store.
her	<u>Her</u> store is in town.
your	<u>Your</u> father is a doctor.
his	<u>His</u> office has blue walls.
its	<u>Its</u> rooms are big.
our	<u>Our</u> parents are busy.
their	<u>Their</u> jobs are interesting.

Read each pair of sentences. Choose the possessive pronoun that belongs in each blank space.

1. Steve is a farmer.
____ farm has many cows.   (His, Her)

2. Laura works for Steve.
____ job is to feed the animals.   (His, Her)

3. The horses are hungry.
____ food is in the barn.   (Our, Their)

Skills Practice

Read each pair of sentences. Write the second sentence. Use the correct pronoun.

1. I work in a library.
____ job is to put away the books.   (Their, My)

2. You live in Greenville.
____ town has a bigger library.   (Your, His)

3. Greenville is a city.
____ streets are busy.   (Its, Our)

4. My family lives in Ohio.
____ town is quiet.   (Its, Our)

5. I have a dog.
____ dog does tricks.   (Your, My)

6. Jorge has a cat.
____ cat sleeps all day.   (His, Her)

Sample Answer **1.** My job is to put away the books.

Skills Review

Read each sentence. Write each pronoun.

1. I cleaned the room.
2. She washed the windows.
3. They looked very dirty.
4. He dusted the table.
5. It needed a tablecloth.
6. We worked hard.
7. You can finish the job.

Read each pair of sentences. Write the correct
pronoun for the second sentence.

8. Jo made a pot.
   ____ used clay.

9. Dan painted the pot.
   ____ used red paint.

10. The pot looked empty.
    ____ needed something.

11. Joe and Dan had two seeds.
    ____ put seeds in the pot.

12. Dan added water.
    ____ filled the pot.

13. Jo put the pot down.
    ____ cleaned up.

Use the correct verb in each sentence. Write the
verb.

14. She ____ music.   (teach, teaches)
15. He ____ the drums.   (play, plays)
16. You ____ the piano.   (play, plays)
17. We ____ the band today at noon.   (join, joins)
18. They ____ our music.   (like, likes)
19. I ____ singing.   (enjoy, enjoys)

Read each pair of sentences. Write the second sentence using the correct pronoun.

20. Mr. Ramos works hard.

_____ job is important.   (Our, His)

21. Ms. Ria goes to the bank.

_____ money is there.   (Her, Their)

22. We have a bank, too.

_____ bank is small.   (Our, Its)

23. Ms. Ames bakes.

_____ bread is hot.   (Her, Your)

24. Bakers sell rolls, too.

_____ rolls sell quickly.   (Our, Their)

25. That cake looks good.

_____ frosting is pink.   (Our, Its)

There are many words that sound the same. But they do not mean the same thing. Look at these words.

<u>Our</u> bus comes in an <u>hour</u>.
<u>We</u> saw a tiny, <u>wee</u> flower.
<u>I</u> have something in my <u>eye</u>.

Can you think of others?

Exploring Language

Alphabetical Order in a Dictionary

Sometimes you need to look up words in a dictionary. You can find words quickly if you know how to use a dictionary. The words in a dictionary are put in alphabetical order. *Alphabetical order* means that words are placed in the same order as the letters of the alphabet.

A B C D E F G H I J K L M N O P Q R S T U V W X Y Z

- Look at the three words in each list. All the words have the same first letter. But they have different second letters. Look at the alphabet. Are these words in alphabetical order?

ladder	smell	game
leak	scare	glass
lizard	see	give

- Look at the three words in each list. The first two letters of each word are the same. But the third letter of each word is different. Look at the alphabet. Are these words in alphabetical order?

molasses	flutter	cream
money	fleece	cross
mouth	flower	crazy

Talk About It

Put the words in each list in alphabetical order.

1. thirsty   **2.** careless   **3.** peak
   trudge   close   perform
   tan   candle   peck

Skills Practice

Write the words in each list in alphabetical order.

1. skirt   **5.** beef   **9.** wool
   shock   banker   wobble
   simply   boss   worker

2. message   **6.** prize   **10.** relay
   meal   sound   rejoice
   medal   puppet   regular

3. away   **7.** rosy   **11.** egg
   art   rough   eight
   arm   roam   else

4. silver   **8.** slide   **12.** noise
   belong   iron   next
   hour   jet   number

Sample Answer **1.** shock simply skirt

Guide Words in a Dictionary

Alphabetical order in a dictionary helps you find words quickly. The dictionary has another way to help you find words. There are two words at the top of almost every dictionary page. These two words are guide words. *Guide Words* tell the first word and the last word on a dictionary page. All the words on a dictionary page must come between the guide words.

far/father

far ~~sie fuge. Et harund dereud fac thusdoun dsisnit siguio duoo doler revident, sind temper sunt in ordus~~

farewell ~~consaur. et vero sus et a this eligand outio ooague nihil dev itn omnis voluptas assumenda. Jet~~

farm ~~Offce aut tum rerum necessi ot recusand. Itenue aetno rerum hic~~

fashion ~~e repciist. harie ago oun porsing aet animodae nost resne co ot nishovol, oisatias aooess polse~~

fast ~~odioaus olvmuda. Et temen k or nod fbibing gun epular religuar~~

fasten ~~schenderit in voluptate vel y minout, potius fuitan mad ut dike oet noque noner imper ned licidin. umident. In prob pary mimult, potk~~

fat ~~e orget. rios emiue et nebevoi, t to feutor oum posn legum edioaur~~

father ~~melesde non recusand. Its n prefer ondis deierib asperiore rup reer ne ad velh non porsing aot on~~

- Look at the dictionary page. What is the first word on the page? What is the last word? What are the guide words?

- Look at these guide words. Which guide words should you use to find the word *clown*?

cloth/club   **coal/cube**

You should use the guide words **cloth/club.** The word *clown* comes between these guide words.

Talk About It

Here is a part of a dictionary page. What are the guide words? Which of the words below would you find on this page?

telephone/ten

1. teeth
2. television
3. tell
4. temper
5. temperature
6. test

Skills Practice

Read each word at the left. Does it come between the guide words in **a** or **b**? Write the letter of the correct pair of words.

1. doctor **a. dock/dollar**
            b. defend/do

2. shook **a. shoe/short**
            b. sick/sign

3. manner **a. magic/main**
             b. manage/many

4. across **a. ache/act**
             b. about/accept

The guide words on a dictionary page are **day/defend.** Which of these words would you find on the page? Write the words.

5. daze   7. debt   9. deed   11. defend

6. dead   8. deck   10. defeat   12. delay

Sample Answer 1. a

Thank-You Notes

You have learned many things about paragraphs. A paragraph can tell about something that happened. It can describe something, or it can give directions. A paragraph can be used in other ways, too.

Pretend you went to a birthday party. Now you want to thank the person who invited you. You could write a paragraph thanking the person. The paragraph that you write is part of a *thank-you note*.

- Look at this thank-you note.

Notice the parts of the thank-you note. The *date* shows when the note was written. The *greeting* shows to whom the note was written. The *paragraph* thanks the person for what was done or given. The *closing* says "good-by" to the person. The *name* shows who wrote the note.

The paragraph of a thank-you note is written a certain way. The main idea sentence tells what was done or given. It is written first. The first word is indented. The detail sentences tell why you liked the event or gift.

Talking About Thank-You Notes

Read the thank-you note on the other page.

1. What is the date?
2. Whose name is in the greeting?
3. What was she thanked for?
4. Who wrote the note?
5. What did she like about the party?
6. What closing did she use?

Writing a Thank-You Note

Read these sentences. They are the paragraph part of a thank-you note. The sentences are not in the right order. Put the sentences in the right order. Write the paragraph. The main idea sentence is *Thank you for the pen you gave me.* Remember to indent the first word.

It will come in handy in school.
After school I write letters to my friends.
School is where I take a lot of tests.
I can also use the pen after school.

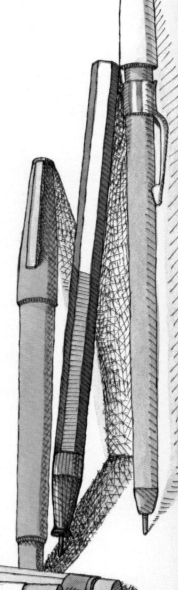

A Class Thank-You Note

Thinking About Thank-You Notes

Your class is going to write a thank-you note together. Pretend that a bus driver visited your class. Now you want to thank her for coming. Your teacher can write your thank-you note on the board.

Writing a Thank-You Note

1. Your thank-you note will begin with today's date.

2. Choose a name to go in the greeting.

3. Start your paragraph with this sentence: *Thank you for visiting our class.*

4. Think of a sentence that tells about what the person does.

5. Think of two more sentences that tell what you learned from the person.

6. For the closing, use *Your friends,*.

7. For the name use ___ *'s class.* Put your teacher's name in the blank.

Your Own Thank-You Note

Thinking About Your Thank-You Note

Now you are going to write your own thank-you note. Pretend you have an Uncle Ted who has given you a bicycle. You want to thank him for it.

Writing Your Thank-You Note

1. Write today's date at the top of your note.

2. Write the greeting: *Dear Uncle Ted,*.

3. Start your paragraph with this sentence: *Thank you for the bicycle you gave me.*

4. Write a sentence telling what you like best about the bike. Use the Word Bank.

5. Write two more sentences telling about places where you can ride.

6. For the closing, write *Love,*.

7. Write your first name.

Word Bank

I
bicycle
speeds
tires
house
store
park

Edit Your Thank-You Note

1. Do your detail sentences tell why you liked the bike?

2. Did you use any pronouns? Which ones did you use?

3. Are the date, greeting, closing, and your name in the right places?

4. Did you indent the first word in the paragraph?

5. Did you use capital letters, commas, and periods correctly?

Introductions

Thinking About Introductions

What happens when a new person comes to your class? Your teacher may tell you the person's name and a little about the person. This is called an introduction. An *introduction* is a way to help people meet each other.

You may introduce people sometimes. You may introduce a new friend to your family. You may introduce a new friend to someone you already know. Introductions are easy when you follow a few rules.

● Look at the pictures to see how Jerry introduced his new friend Sam to his sister Peg.

Jerry did a good job of introducing Sam to Peg. Jerry told Peg a little bit about Sam in the introduction. He also told Sam who Peg was.

Talking About Introductions

Pretend you have brought a new friend home to introduce to your family. Your friend's name is Amy. She has just moved to your neighborhood from another town. You are going to introduce Amy to your brother Bob.

1. Choose two people to introduce to each other. One of them will be Amy. The other one will be Bob.

2. Introduce Amy to Bob. Tell Bob something about Amy in the introduction. Tell Amy who Bob is.

3. Let Bob and Amy speak to each other after you have introduced them.

Careers

Would you like to run a supermarket? You will have many jobs to do. Writing and speaking skills will be important. Sometimes you will need to order food. You must be able to write orders that are easy to understand. Many people will work for you. You must give them clear directions. People who shop in your store will ask many questions. You will have to answer each question.

Robert Houser

Conversations

When you talk with someone else, you have a
conversation. In a conversation, you say things to
another person. You also listen to what the other
person says to you.

Sometimes you want to write a conversation.
You use a special way of writing. You put *quotation
marks* around the words that each person says.
You use a *conversation word* such as *said, whispered,*
or *called* to tell how the person talked. You *indent*
the first word each time a new person talks.

● Read this conversation between Joey and Gail.

Joey said, "My uncle is a builder. He
built the green house across the street."

Gail answered, "My aunt also builds
houses. She built the house she lives in."

Joey added, "Next month my uncle
will help put up the new library."

Gail cried, "I think my aunt plans to
work on the library, too."

Talking About a Conversation

Look at the conversation again.

1. Where are quotation marks used in the conversation?
2. What conversation words show how Joey and Gail talked?
3. How many times is the first word indented in the conversation?
4. Which person talked first in the conversation?
5. Did Joey and Gail listen to each other in their conversation? How do you know?

Below is a cartoon. It shows Joey and Gail talking again. They might be talking about what happened in school that day. They might be talking about a class trip to the zoo.

Look at each box. Who is talking? What do you think each person is saying?

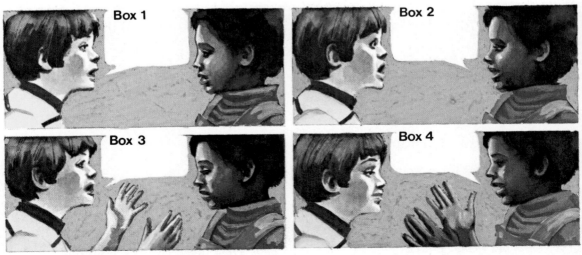

Box 1

Box 2

Box 3

Box 4

Checking Skills

Some special signs are missing in each sentence. Write each sentence correctly. *pages 108-109*

1. a dentist fixes teeth
2. who is your dentist
3. what a big chair he has
4. can we go now

Write each sentence. Draw a line between the subject part and the predicate part. *pages 110-111*

5. Amy delivers newspapers.
6. My father got a letter.
7. Howard fights fires.
8. The bell rings loudly.

Write each sentence. Draw one line under each noun. Draw two lines under each verb. *pages 112-113*

9. The girl cuts the grass.
10. A boy waters the plants.
11. The garden needs a fence.
12. The children plant beans.

Look at the underlined words. Use the correct pronoun to take their place. Write the new sentence. *pages 116-117*

13. Rudy cleans his room.
    ___ sweeps the floor.
14. Diane makes her bed.
    ___ dusts her chair.
15. Rudy and Diana jump rope.
    ___ sing a song.
16. The day is very cool.
    ___ is dark.

Use the correct verb in each sentence. Write the verb. *pages 118-119*

17. You ___ music.   (teach, teaches)
18. I ___ the drums.   (play, plays)

19. She ___ to take lessons. (want, wants)

20. He ___ very fast. (learn, learns)

Read each pair of sentences. Write the second sentence using the correct pronoun. *pages 120-121*

21. Janet made breakfast.
___ brother helped. (Her, Their)

22. Glen was hungry.
___ plate was full. (Our, His)

23. I was not hungry.
___ plate was not full. (My, Your)

24. Glen and I cleaned up.
___ jobs are done. (Our, Your)

Now you will write a thank-you note. *pages 128-131*

25. The following are the parts of a thank-you note. The parts are not in order. Put the parts in the right order. Then write the thank-you note.

a. Your friend,

b. Dear Maria,

c. Sally

d. October 19, 19 __

e. Thank you for the books you gave me. I have already started the first book. The story is interesting so far. The pictures are also nice.

A Play

A *play* is a story that is acted out. The people in a play have conversations. This story is part of a book called <u>The Adventures of Tom Sawyer</u> by Samuel Clemens. Clemens grew up in Hannibal, Missouri. Read the play carefully.

Tom Sawyer · Fence Washer

CHARACTERS:
Narrator
Aunt Polly
Tom Sawyer
Ben Rogers
Sarah Howard
Janie Miller

NARRATOR: It was Saturday morning in Hannibal, Missouri. Every boy in town was planning a day full of fun and adventure. Every boy, that is, but Tom Sawyer. Aunt Polly had other ideas for him.

AUNT POLLY: Stop playing with that brush and get to work, Tom Sawyer! I expect you to have that fence whitewashed by the time I get back from town.

TOM SAWYER: Yes, Aunt Polly. (*Aunt Polly leaves. Tom looks at the huge fence before him and sighs.*)

TOM: There must be an easy way to do this job.

NARRATOR: Tom began to whitewash. Just then his friend Ben Rogers came walking by. Suddenly Tom got an idea.

BEN ROGERS: It sure is beautiful day to go swimming. Too bad you have to work, Tom.

TOM: Who's working, Ben?

BEN: Why, you are! Don't you call whitewashing a fence work?

TOM: Well, I suppose some people might call it work. But I haven't had so much fun in a long time.

BEN: You mean you *like* it?

TOM: I sure do. It isn't every day a boy gets a chance to whitewash a fence. (*Tom begins to whistle as he works. Ben looks surprised.*)

BEN: Say, Tom, let me whitewash a little.

TOM: Oh, I don't know, Ben. Aunt Polly's awfully particular about this fence.

BEN: Oh, come on, Tom. I'll be careful. I promise.

TOM: I'd like to Ben, but—

BEN: I'll give you this apple I have in my pocket.

TOM: (*taking the apple*) Well, maybe just for a bit.

BEN: (*taking the brush*) Gee, thanks Tom! (*Ben whitewashes and Tom eats the apple. Sarah Howard and Janie Miller enter.*)

SARAH HOWARD: Poor Ben! He has to work today!

BEN: I don't *have* to work. Tom let me.

JANIE MILLER: He *what?*

BEN: I gave him my apple and he let me whitewash.

SARAH: You must be crazy!

BEN: I am not crazy. It isn't every day a boy gets a chance to whitewash a fence. Right, Tom?

TOM: Right, Ben. Now why don't you go on about your business. You're spoiling Ben's fun. (*Sarah and Janie stare at Tom. Then they stare at Ben.*)

SARAH: Hey, Tom, how about giving me a try at whitewashing?

JANIE: Me too!

TOM: Gee, I'd like to but—

SARAH: I'll give you my kite!

JANIE: I'll give you my pet frog!

TOM: Well, I suppose Ben could use a little rest . . .

NARRATOR: So Sarah and Janie took their turns whitewashing the fence. In a few hours the job was done. The painters left just as Aunt Polly arrived home.

AUNT POLLY: Well, I'll be! Tom Sawyer, I'm surprised!

TOM: (*smiling*) Oh, it wasn't so hard a job.

AUNT POLLY: It wasn't?

TOM: No, not after my friends taught me a funny thing. The only difference between work and play is how you look at it.

AUNT POLLY: I must say, Tom, sometimes you say the strangest things!

—*Steven Otfinoski*

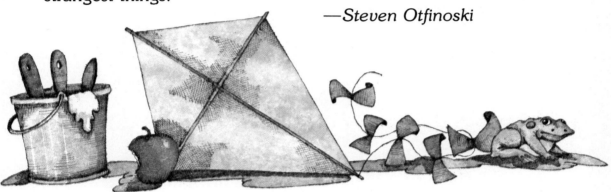

Activities

1. Six students can act out the play in class. Bring the things that are needed, such as a brush and an apple. Practice the play before presenting it to the class.

2. **Creative Writing** Think about the time when you had the most fun ever. Write a paragraph that tells what you did. Tell when and where the action took place.

Mid-Year Review

Read the groups of words in each pair. Write the group of words that is a sentence. *pages 2–3*

1. A dog.
   A dog chased a cat.

2. A cat climbed a tree.
   A cat.

3. A bird.
   A bird caught a worm.

4. An owl slept all day.
   An owl.

Read each sentence. Write **telling** if it is a telling sentence. Write **question** if it is a question sentence. Write **exclamation** if it is an exclamation sentence. *pages 6–7*

5. Ana walked to town.
6. Did she take her dog?
7. How long the walk was!

8. Ana saw two cats.
9. How pretty they were!
10. Did Ana go home?

Some special signs are missing in each sentence. Write each sentence correctly. *pages 8–9*

11. a bird made a nest
12. does the bird sing
13. the bird has feathers

14. how red the feathers are
15. does the bird fly
16. how high it flies

Look at the part in the box. Write **subject** if it is a subject part. Write **predicate** if it is a predicate part. *pages 12–13*

17. The farmer │ gave us a chicken.
18. The chicken │ ran around the yard.
19. The chicken │ scratched for worms.
20. The children │ fed the chicken.

Write the nouns. Write **singular** if the noun is
singular. Write **plural** if the noun is plural. *pages 40-41*

21. Birds sing songs.
22. A boy hit a ball.
23. A girl rode a bike.

24. Boys read books.
25. Dogs chased sticks.
26. A cat chased a toy.

Write the plural form of each singular noun. *pages 42-44*

27. bat
28. box

29. tooth
30. party

31. fly
32. wish

Change the underlined word to tell what kind of
work the person does. Write the second sentence
with the new word. *page 45*

33. Amy <u>sings</u> well.   Amy is a ___.
34. Robin <u>teaches</u> school.   Robin is a ___.
35. Joan <u>writes</u> books.   Joan is a ___.
36. Juan <u>builds</u> houses.   Juan is a ___.

Write each noun. Write **proper** if the noun is a
proper noun. Write **common** if it is a common noun. *pages 48-49*

37. Ed flew to Texas.
38. A car went to Dallas.
39. Cows stood by the road.

40. Ed went to Trees Road.
41. Miyo waved at Ed.
42. Miyo opened the door.

Write each name and address correctly. *pages 50-53*

43.
ms judith s levine
2 astor court
augusta maine 04330

44.
miss noreen sullivan
280 beacon street
provo utah 84601

Mid-Year Review

Write each date correctly. *pages 50-53*

45. September 9 1980   **48.** June 12 1981
46. November 10 1982   **49.** March 6 1982
47. October 14 1982   **50.** January 18 1979

Read each sentence. Write the correct verb. *pages 76-77*

51. Felipe ____ a rock garden   (build, builds)
52. He ____ for pretty rocks.   (search, searches)
53. Christine ____ some rocks.   (carry, carries)
54. They ____ flowers by the rocks.   (plant, plants)
55. Some children ____ in the pool.   (swim, swims)
56. They ____ water on Felipe.   (splash, splashes)

Read each sentence. Write the verb in the present. *pages 78-79*

57. Christine ____ a tree.   (climb)
58. Christine ____ a tiny bird.   (see)
59. The tiny bird ____ on a tiny twig.   (sit)
60. Christine and Leo ____ for a nest.   (look)
61. They ____ a squirrel.   (find)
62. They ____ the squirrel.   (watch)

Read each sentence. Write the verb in the past. *pages 84-85*

63. Holly ____ a butterfly.   (chase)
64. The butterfly ____ away.   (hurry)
65. Leo ____ the dog.   (wash)
66. The children ____ some sandwiches.   (carry)
67. They ____ their lunch.   (pack)
68. The boys ____ the dishes.   (dry)

Write each sentence. Draw a line between the
subject part and the predicate part. *pages 110-111*

69. The ship sails.
70. Sailors work.

71. The wind blows.
72. Many sailors sing.

Write each sentence. Draw one line under each
noun. Draw two lines under each verb. *pages 112-113*

73. Hao arrived in Paris.
74. Ann opened her window.
75. A man chased his hat.

76. A dog barked at Tom.
77. The women walked up the steps.
78. The birds stayed in the nest.

Complete each sentence that has a blank. Write
the pronoun. *pages 116-117, 120-121*

79. John grows a garden.
____ planted daisies.
80. Maria runs a shop.
____ sells hats.

81. The rain falls.
____ floods the street.
82. Farmers clean the barn.
____ feed animals, too.

83. The children listen to a ghost story.
____ teacher reads the story.   (Their, Its)
84. ____ voice is low.   (Its, Her)
85. ____ sound scares William.   (Its, Their)
86. ____ eyes get bigger.   (Our, His)

Write the correct verb for each sentence. *pages 118-119*

87. She ____ a tractor.   (drive, drives)
88. They ____ bridges.   (build, builds)
89. He ____ watches.   (repair, repairs)
90. I ____ in a group.   (sing, sings)

Grammar and Related Language Skills

Review of Nouns
Possessive Nouns
Sentence Building
Capitalizing Proper Nouns

Practical Communication

Using a Dictionary
Writing a Friendly Letter

Creative Expression

A Poem

Reviewing Nouns

You have learned that nouns are naming words. Words like *child, forest,* and *tree* are nouns.

> A **noun** is a word that names a person, a place, or a thing.

You know that nouns can name one or more than one thing. The noun *flower* names one thing. The noun *flowers* names more than one thing.

> A **singular noun** is a noun that names one person, place, or thing.

> A **plural noun** is a noun that names more than one person, place, or thing. Most plural nouns have **s** or **es** endings.

You have learned about different kinds of nouns. The noun *girl* names any girl. The noun *Nancy* names a special girl.

> A **common noun** is a noun that names any person, place, or thing.

> A **proper noun** is a noun that names a special person, place, or thing. Each important word in a proper noun begins with a capital letter.

● Read each sentence. Then read each noun. Is it singular or plural? Is it a common noun or a proper noun?

David went to Jones Beach.   The ocean had big waves.

Read these sentences. Find each noun. Is the noun singular or plural? Is it a common noun or a proper noun?

1. Carla gathers shells.
2. A shell lies in the sand.
3. A turtle crawls out.
4. Sand Beach looks clean.

Skills Practice _____

Read these sentences. Write each noun. Write **singular** if the noun is singular. Write **plural** if the noun is plural.

1. Two boys see a fish.
2. The fish has blue eyes.
3. The fish has a blue tail.
4. A girl swims.
5. The girl sees big rocks.
6. The rocks hide a fish.

Write each sentence correctly. Use a capital letter to begin each important word in a proper noun.

7. Our class saw mrs. lee.
8. Does peter swim often?
9. Pilar lives on main street.
10. A dog sees juan lopez.
11. Sometimes mary swims.
12. Did mr. arias see a fish?

Writing Sentences _____

Pretend you are playing at the beach.

1. Think of a singular noun. Use it in a sentence.
2. Think of a plural noun. Use it in a sentence.
3. Think of a proper noun. Use it in a sentence.

Sample Answers 1. boys, plural; fish, singular **7.** Our class saw Mrs. Lee.

Possessive Nouns

Read this sentence.

A *turtle's shell* makes a good house.

When you talk about a *turtle's shell,* you are talking about something that *belongs to* a turtle. You use a special form of the noun *turtle* to show that the turtle has a shell. The word *turtle's* is called a possessive noun.

> A **possessive noun** is a noun that names who or what has something.

● Read each sentence. Find the possessive noun.

The snake's skin shines in the sun.
The duck's feathers are white.
The frog's mouth opened wide.
A fish's tail waved in the water.

Talk About It

Read each sentence. What is the possessive noun?

1. Linda's snake lived under a rock.
2. Now the box is the snake's home.
3. Andy's frog jumps high in the air.
4. The frog's back has green spots.

Skills Practice

Write each sentence. Draw one line under the possessive noun.

1. Mr. Chin's mouse has a long tail.
2. The mouse's fur is white.
3. Mrs. Brown's fish swims in a bowl.
4. The fish's mother lived in a pond.
5. We found a robin's nest.
6. A branch held the bird's nest.
7. The robin's nest had three eggs.
8. A little bird's head appeared.
9. We heard the baby's cry.
10. The bird's mother will bring food soon.

Sample Answer 1. <u>Mr. Chin's</u> mouse has a long tail.

Forming Singular Possessive Nouns

You know that possessive nouns name who or what has something.

Ellen's horse won the race.

Ellen is a singular noun that names one person. To show that something belongs to Ellen, you write *Ellen's*. You add an *apostrophe* and *s ('s)*.

Ellen + 's ⟶ Ellen's

• Look at each pair of nouns. What was added to each singular noun to make it possessive?

sister	Jason	bird
sister's	Jason's	bird's

Add an **apostrophe** and **s ('s)** to write the possessive of most singular nouns.

Talk About It

What is the possessive form of each singular noun? Use each possessive noun in a sentence.

1. fish   **2.** hen   **3.** Bonnie   **4.** brother

Skills Practice

Write the possessive form of each singular noun.

1. goose   **3.** Glen   **5.** squirrel   **7.** boy
2. Diane   **4.** bug   **6.** girl   **8.** owl

Sample Answer **1.** goose's

Forming Plural Possessive Nouns

You can make plural nouns possessive, too.

The farmers' tractor stopped.

The word *farmers* is a plural noun that ends in *s*.
To show that something belongs to the farmers, you
write *farmers'*. You add an *apostrophe* (').

farmers + ' ——→ farmers'

● Look at each pair of nouns. What was added to
each plural noun to make it possessive?

ducks   ants   daughters
ducks'   ants'   daughters'

> Add an **apostrophe** (') to write the
> possessive of most plural nouns.

Talk About It

What is the possessive form of each plural noun?
Use each possessive noun in a sentence.

1. girls   **2.** teachers   **3.** skunks   **4.** horses

Skills Practice

Write the possessive of each plural noun.

1. animals   **3.** doctors   **5.** rabbits   **7.** frogs
2. boys   **4.** raccoons   **6.** friends   **8.** sons

Sample Answer **1.** animals'

Possessive Nouns in Sentences

You use possessive nouns to name who or what has something. Possessive nouns can be singular or plural.

The <u>boy's dogs</u> bark.   The <u>boys' dogs</u> bark.

Boy's is a singular possessive noun. It shows that one person has the dogs.
Boys' is a plural possessive noun. It shows that more than one person has the dogs.

● Read each sentence. Find the possessive noun. Is it singular or plural? What ending was added to make the noun possessive?

The girls followed the animal's tracks.
They led to a bear's cave.
The girls' brother called them.
He found a raccoon's tracks.

Talk About It

Complete each sentence. Decide if the noun in ( ) is singular or plural. Then use the possessive form of the noun in the blank.

1. The ____ cat has two kittens.   (boy)
2. They sleep in the ____ basket.   (cat)
3. The ____ mother feeds them.   (kittens)
4. The ____ friend took a kitten.   (girls)

Skills Practice

Decide if the noun in ( ) is singular or plural. Use the possessive form of the noun in the blank. Write the sentence.

1. The ____ dog chased a rabbit.   (boys)
2. The ____ tail wagged.   (dog)
3. The dog ran to the ____ home.   (rabbit)
4. The rabbit hid in the ____ tent.   (girls)
5. The boys saw a ____ nest in a tree.   (squirrel)
6. Some squirrels ate the ____ popcorn.   (boys)
7. A squirrel ran across a ____ tent.   (girl)

Writing Sentences

Pretend you and a friend are walking in a forest. Think of some animals you might see. Write two sentences to tell about them. Use a possessive noun in each sentence.

Sample Answers **1.** The boys' dog chased a rabbit. **2.** The dog's tail wagged.

Skills Review

Read these sentences. Write each noun. Write
singular if the noun is singular. Write **plural** if the
noun is plural.

1. The rabbit has long ears.
2. Rabbits eat green plants.
3. The fox chases the squirrel.
4. Squirrels hide nuts in trees.
5. The owl lives in a tree.
6. Owls fly at night.

Write each sentence correctly. Use a capital letter
to begin each important word in a proper noun.

7. Did mr. black pick some flowers?
8. My aunt gave the pretty rock to mrs. ramos.
9. Does jane like animals?
10. My sister visited a friend in new mexico.
11. The turtle belongs to barry.

Read these sentences. Write the possessive nouns.

12. Paul's dog barks.
13. He pats the dog's head.
14. The dog runs to Jill's house.
15. She rides a friend's horse.
16. The horse's legs are white.

Write the possessive form of each singular noun.

17. Jack
18. raccoon
19. puppy
20. girl

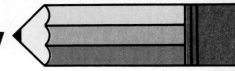

Write the possessive form of each plural noun.

21. kittens   **23.** owls
22. boys   **24.** bears

Decide if the noun in ( ) is singular or plural. Use the possessive form of the noun in the blank. Write the possessive form of each noun.

25. We found an ____ tracks.   (animal)
26. They led to the ____ tent.   (boys)
27. A ____ paws made the track.   (raccoon)
28. The raccoon ate the ____ popcorn.   (girls)
29. A ____ bark scared the raccoon.   (dog)

**In Spanish, you say
—El vestido de Rosa es rojo.
(The dress of Rosa is red.)**

**In English, you say
—Rosa's dress is red.
There are no possessive nouns in Spanish. The word *de* shows that the dress belongs to Rosa. What shows the same thing in English?**

Exploring
Language

Possessive Nouns
with Special Endings

Some plural nouns do not form the plural in the usual way. They do not end in *s* or *es*.

- Read each pair of nouns below. Which noun is singular? Which noun is plural? Look at how the spelling in the plural noun changes.

SINGULAR	man	woman	child	mouse	goose
PLURAL	men	women	children	mice	geese

The plural nouns in the boxes do not end in *s*. Suppose you want to show that something belongs to the men. You add an *apostrophe* and *s ('s)*.

The men's voices are loud.

All the plural nouns above work the same way. You add an *apostrophe* and *s ('s)* to make the nouns possessive.

- Read each sentence. Find the possessive noun. How was each possessive noun formed?

The children's pet mouse lives in a cage.
A kitten ate the mice's food.
The women's geese are in the lake.
We hear the geese's cries.

Talk About It

Complete each sentence. Look at the noun in ( ).
Use the possessive form of the noun in the blank.

1. The ___ father bought a puppy. (child)
2. The puppy played with the ___ dog. (man)
3. The ___ dogs liked each other. (men)

Skills Practice

Look at the noun in ( ). Use the possessive
form of the noun in the blank. Write each
sentence.

1. The ___ bird sang a song. (woman)
2. The ___ mother fed the birds. (children)
3. A young ___ feathers are soft. (goose)
4. The ___ dog found a fox. (men)
5. The fox tried to hide in a ___ hole. (mouse)
6. The ___ friend called the dog. (child)
7. We kept bags of seed in the ___ barn. (women)
8. We saw the ___ nest in the barn. (mice)
9. The seed was for the ___ geese. (man)
10. The mice ate the ___ food. (geese)

Sample Answers **1.** The woman's bird sang a song.
2. The children's mother fed the birds.

Writing Sentences

You can put together sentences like these to make one sentence.

| Frank has a raccoon.
 The raccoon eats corn. | → | Frank's raccoon eats corn. |

The new sentence tells the same thing. But it does not use the same words over again. You use a possessive noun in the new sentence.

- Read the two groups of words again. What word in the new sentence shows that Frank has a raccoon? What kind of word is it?

Talk About It

Read each pair of sentences. Put them together to make one sentence. What possessive noun did you use in the new sentence?

1. Ned has a pony
The pony has spots.

2. The boys have a wagon.
The wagon has wheels.

Skills Practice

Read each pair of sentences. Put them together to make one sentence. Write the new sentence.

1. Pam has a fish.
The fish lives in a bowl.

2. Elisa has a turtle.
The turtle walks slowly.

3. The girls have horses.
The horses trot quickly.

4. Mr. Li has mice.
The mice make noise.

Sample Answer **1.** Pam's fish lives in a bowl.

Compound Words

Words change all the time. New words are made up. Some old words are no longer used. One way to make a new word is to put two words together. A *compound word* is a word made up of two other words.

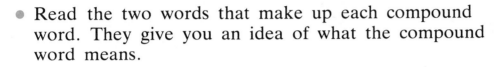

homework ⟶ home + work
tablecloth ⟶ table + cloth

- Read the two words that make up each compound word. They give you an idea of what the compound word means.

Homework is <u>work</u> you do at <u>home</u>.
A <u>tablecloth</u> is a <u>cloth</u> you put on a <u>table</u>.

Talk About It

What two words make up each compound word?
Use them to tell the meaning of the compound word.

1. doghouse   **2.** football   **3.** birthday   **4.** spaceship

Skills Practice

Find the two words that make up each compound word. Use them in the blanks to tell the meaning of the compound word. Then write each sentence.

1. A <u>basketball</u> is a ___ you throw through a ___ .
2. A <u>sailboat</u> is a ___ with a ___ .
3. A <u>raincoat</u> is a ___ you wear in the ___ .
4. A <u>lunchroom</u> is a ___ where you eat ___ .

Sample Answer 1. A basketball is a ball you throw through a basket.

Writing Days, Months, and Special Days

You know that you should start each proper noun with a capital letter. The names of days, months, and special days are proper nouns. They begin with capital letters.

DAYS OF THE WEEK	MONTHS OF THE YEAR	SPECIAL DAYS
Sunday	January	New Year's Day
Monday	February	Lincoln's Birthday
Tuesday	March	Washington's Birthday
Wednesday	April	April Fools' Day
Thursday	May	Mother's Day
Friday	June	Father's Day
Saturday	July	Independence Day
	August	Halloween
	September	Thanksgiving
	October	Labor Day
	November	
	December	

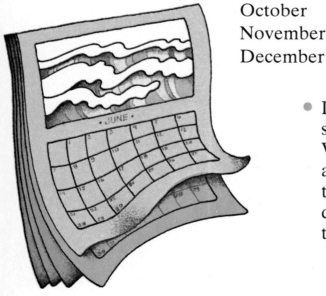

- Look at the list of special days above. Which names have apostrophes? Can you think of other special days? How do you write them?

Talk About It

Read these sentences. What words should begin with capital letters?

1. The first day in january is new year's day.
2. Is labor day always on monday?
3. Which day in july is independence day?
4. When is washington's birthday?

Skills Practice

Write each sentence correctly. Use a capital letter to begin each important word in a proper noun.

1. My family went on vacation in august.
2. Is lincoln's birthday in february?
3. Do you go to school on saturday?
4. We go to the library every tuesday.
5. I dress up on halloween.
6. Do you like april fools' day?
7. We have mother's day in may.
8. Is father's day in june?
9. Our thanksgiving day is always on thursday.
10. We played outside on sunday.

Writing Sentences

Think about your three favorite special days. Write a sentence to tell what you do on each special day.

Sample Answer 1. My family went on vacation in August.

Skills Review

Look at the noun in ( ). Use the possessive form of the noun in the blank. Write the possessive form of each noun.

1. The ___ cow gives milk.   (woman)
2. The ___ horses eat hay.   (men)
3. The ___ cat sleeps in the barn.   (child)
4. The ___ babies are tiny.   (mouse)
5. The ___ dog wants a bone.   (children)
6. The ___ chickens laid many eggs.   (women)

Read each pair of sentences. Put them together to make one sentence. Write the new sentence.

7. Mark has a tent.
   The tent keeps out the rain.

8. Mr. Silver has a dog.
   The dog chases rabbits.

9. The boys have friends.
   The friends like to swim.

10. Ms. Olson has a pond.
    The pond has many fish.

11. The girls have a bird.
    The bird can talk.

12. Ann has a cat.
    The cat lives in the barn.

Find the two words that make up each compound word. Use them in the blanks to tell the meaning of the compound word. Then write each sentence.

13. A <u>tablecloth</u> is a ___ you put on a ___ .
14. A <u>doghouse</u> is a ___ for a ___ .
15. A <u>sailboat</u> is a ___ with a ___ .
16. A <u>football</u> is a ___ you kick with your ___ .
17. A <u>spaceship</u> is a ___ that goes into ___ .

Write each sentence correctly. Use a capital letter to begin each important word in a proper noun.

18. We have chicken for dinner on wednesday.
19. It can be very windy in march.
20. I bought my bike in december.
21. We have thanksgiving day in november.
22. It often rains in april.
23. We went on vacation in september.
24. They stayed home on sunday.
25. Is halloween in october?

Read this verse. What does the verse tell you about the different months of the year?

Thirty days have September,
April, June, and November,
All the rest have thirty-one,
Except for February alone,
Which has but twenty-eight in time
Till Leap Year gives it twenty-nine.

Exploring
Language

Dictionary: Word Meaning

You find new words in many different places. You may read new words in books. Sometimes you hear people use new words when they talk. A dictionary can help you find out what the words mean.

- Look at this dictionary page. Find the word *dodo*. What does *dodo* mean?

---

do/dot

do   Susan helped Mary *do* her homework.

doctor   Someone who takes care of sick people and makes them well. Sara's father took her to the *doctor* when she was sick.

dodo   A kind of large bird that lived a long time ago. The *dodo* had a big hooked bill and a short tail of curly feathers. Its wings were so small that the bird could not fly.

dog   An animal that has four legs, fur, and barks. Leroy has a *dog* as a pet.

doll   A toy that looks like a baby, a child, or an older person.

dollar   A piece of money. It is the same as one hundred cents.

donkey   An animal that looks very much like a small horse. It sometimes carries or pulls things. The *donkey* pulled the wagon.

dot   A small, round mark or spot. This dress has many *dots*.

Sometimes you find an example sentence after a word meaning. The *example sentence* shows you how the word is used.

- Use the dictionary page above. Find the word *donkey*. What does *donkey* mean? Read the example sentence for *donkey*.

Talk About It _____

Find these words on the sample dictionary page.
Tell the meaning of each word.

1. dollar   **2.** doctor   **3.** doll

Complete each sentence. Choose the correct word
from the sample dictionary page.

4. Ms. Ramos gave me a ___ for helping her.
5. That ___ looks like a real baby.

Skills Practice _____

Find these words on the sample dictionary page.
Write the meaning of each word.

1. dot   **2.** dog   **3.** do

Look at each picture. Find the words on the sample
dictionary page that name what each picture shows.
Write the words.

4.   **5.**   **6.**

Complete each sentence. Choose the correct word
from the sample dictionary page. Write the word.

7. Pete's ___ always barks at me.
8. The ___ carried heavy boxes.
9. Don helped me ___ a trick.
10. My new dress has many blue ___ .

Sample Answers 1. A small, round mark or spot. **7.** dog

Dictionary: Words with Two Meanings

You can use a dictionary to find out what a word means. Sometimes a word can have two meanings. Then the dictionary tells both meanings. You will find **1.** in front of the first meaning. You will find **2.** in front of the second meaning.

- Look at this dictionary page. Find the word *draw*. What are the two meanings of *draw*?

---

dance/dust

dance **1.** To move the feet or body in time to music. Do you like to *dance*? **2.** A party where people dance. Susan and John are going to a *dance* tonight.

dart **1.** To move suddenly or quickly. The fox *darted* into the bushes. **2.** Something thin and pointed that looks like a small arrow.

date **1.** The day, month, year, or time when something happens. **2.** A sweet fruit that grows on a tree. Henry likes *dates* better than candy.

draw **1.** To make a picture of something. My teacher asked me to *draw* a picture of a balloon. **2.** To move something in a direction. The farmer used a donkey to *draw* her wagon.

dress **1.** To put on things to wear. Will you *dress* Carmen's new doll? **2.** Something girls and women wear. My mother bought me a *dress*.

dust **1.** Tiny pieces of earth or dirt. The rain cleared the *dust* from the air. **2.** To clean off something. Tony's brother will *dust* the tables.

- Read this sentence. Which meaning of *draw* fits this sentence?

The pony <u>draws</u> a small red cart.

Talk About It

Read each sentence. Use the sample dictionary page. Tell which meaning of *dart* fits each sentence.

1. They aimed the <u>darts</u> at the dart board.
2. The cat <u>darted</u> behind a fence.

Skills Practice

Look at the underlined word in each sentence. Use the sample dictionary page. Write **1.** if the word has the first meaning. Write **2.** if the word has the second meaning.

1. We made a bread out of <u>dates</u>.
2. The dolls <u>dance</u> on the music box.
3. I must <u>dust</u> all the old books.
4. What is the <u>date</u> of your birthday?
5. The <u>dust</u> made me sneeze.
6. I will <u>draw</u> a picture of the plane.
7. My best <u>dress</u> is too small now.

Sample Answer 1. 2.

A Friendly Letter

Thinking About a Letter

Most people like being with their friends. They want to tell about interesting things that have happened to them. They also like to hear what their friends are doing.

Sometimes friends move away. But you still like to share news with them. That is why you write friendly letters. A *friendly letter* is a way to tell your friends what you are doing.

● Look at the letter Mark wrote to a friend who had moved away.

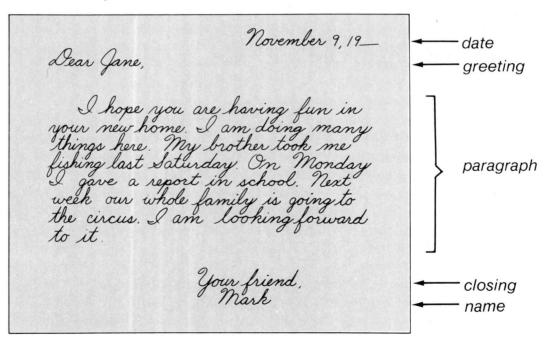

November 9, 19___ ← date

Dear Jane, ← greeting

I hope you are having fun in your new home. I am doing many things here. My brother took me fishing last Saturday. On Monday I gave a report in school. Next week our whole family is going to the circus. I am looking forward to it. } paragraph

Your friend, ← closing
Mark ← name

In the paragraph Mark told about things that happened to him. He said the same things he might say if he were talking to his friend in person.

A friendly letter and a thank-you note have the same parts. Mark's letter has a *date,* a *greeting,* a *paragraph,* a *closing,* and the writer's *name.*

Remember what each part of the letter does.

Date. Shows when the letter was written
Greeting. Shows to whom the letter was written
Paragraph. Tells the person something
Closing. Says "good-by" to the person
Name. Shows who wrote the letter

Commas are used in the date, greeting, and closing. Remember to indent the first word of the paragraph.

Talking About a Letter

Read the letter on the other page.
1. Who wrote the letter?
2. What was the date?
3. Whose name was in the greeting?
4. What was the closing?
5. What did the writer talk about in the letter?
6. Where were commas used in the letter?

Writing a Letter

When you write a friendly letter, you need to know what order the parts come in. The parts of a friendly letter are listed below. They are not in the order you would write them. Write the parts in the correct order.

name	date	greeting
paragraph	closing	

A Class Letter

Thinking About Letters

Your class is going to write a friendly letter together. Pretend that someone in your class is ill. The person has been out of school for a week. Your class wants to write to him or her and tell what is happening in school.

When you finish writing a letter, you need to address an envelope to send your letter. Here is the way an envelope is addressed:

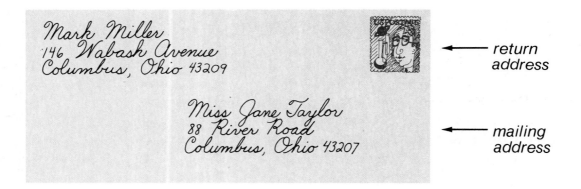

Mark Miller
146 Wabash Avenue
Columbus, Ohio 43209 ← *return address*

Miss Jane Taylor
88 River Road
Columbus, Ohio 43207 ← *mailing address*

The middle of the envelope has the *mailing address*. This is the name and address of the person who will get the letter.

The top left corner of the envelope has the *return address*. It shows the writer's name and address. If the post office cannot find the house of the person to whom the letter is written, they will return the letter to the writer.

Remember to use capital letters for the names of people, streets, cities, and states. There is a comma between the city and state. The ZIP code follows the state.

Writing a Letter

Your teacher will write the letter and envelope on the board.

1. Begin the letter with today's date.
2. Use the greeting *Dear Bill,*. Where should it be written?
3. Start your paragraph with this sentence: *We hope you are feeling better.*
4. Think of one sentence that tells about what happened in class yesterday.
5. Think of a sentence that tells about your homework. Think of another sentence about what will happen in class tomorrow.
6. Use the closing *Your friends,*.
7. For the name, use ____ *'s class.* Use your teacher's name in the blank.
8. Think of a mailing address and a return address for the envelope.

Careers

Forest rangers have an important job. They take care of plants and animals in our parks and forests. They watch for fires and floods. They must read books to learn how to take care of our forests. Forest rangers also must speak well. They guide people through our parks and forests. They tell the visitors about plants and animals.

Robert Houser

Your Own Friendly Letter

Thinking About Your Letter

Now you are going to write your own friendly letter. Pretend that a friend has moved away. You want to write to him or her. In the letter you can tell about how you spent Valentine's Day at school. You may also tell about something else.

The pictures below will help you. They show some of the things you might do in class. The Word Bank can help you, too. It shows how to spell some of the words you may want to use.

Writing Your Letter

1. Begin your letter with today's date.
2. Use the name of a real friend in your greeting. Write the word *Dear* before your friend's name. Use a comma after the name.
3. Start your paragraph with this sentence: *I had a good time on Valentine's Day.* You may also use your own sentence.

4. Write one sentence telling how you made a mailbox for valentines.

5. Write one sentence telling about one boy's valentine.

6. Write one sentence telling about two girls' valentines.

7. Use the closing *Your friend,*. Write your own name after the closing.

8. Address an envelope to send your letter in.
Write a name and mailing address.
Use your own name and address for the
return address.

Edit Your Letter

Edit your letter and envelope. Use the questions below.

1. Did your detail sentences tell about the pictures?

2. Which possessive nouns did you use in your sentences?

3. Are the date, greeting, closing, and name in the right places? Did you use commas correctly?

4. Did you capitalize the names of people, months, streets, cities, states, and special days?

5. Is your envelope addressed correctly? Correct your mistakes. Make a good copy of your letter and envelope.

Checking Skills

Read these sentences. Write each noun. Write **singular** if the noun is singular. Write **plural** if the noun is plural. *pages 148-149*

1. The man found a cave.
2. The cave had two cubs.
3. Two lions came to the cave.
4. The lions brought food.

Write each sentence correctly. Use a capital letter to begin each important word in a proper noun. *pages 148-149*

5. mr. alba watched the rain.
6. He was inside lincoln school.
7. leah wanted to go outside.
8. People ran down liberty avenue.

Read these sentences. Write the possessive nouns. *pages 150-151*

9. We drove past Judy's house.
10. Maria's brother waved to us.
11. A man's dog barked at me.
12. My friend's dog barked, too.

Decide if the noun in ( ) is singular or plural. Write the possessive form of each noun. *pages 154-155*

13. The ___ frog is green. (boys)
14. The ___ legs are strong. (frog)
15. The frog can jump out of the ___ box. (girl)
16. My ___ cat saw the frog. (friends)

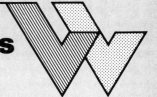

Look at the noun at the end of each sentence. Write the possessive form of each noun. *pages 158-159*

17. We found the ___ nest. (mice)
18. The ___ friends waited outside. (children)
19. I have the ___ hat. (man)
20. They touch the ___ feathers. (geese)

Read each pair of sentences. Put them together to make one sentence. Write the new sentence. *page 160*

21. George has a kite.
The kite is red.

22. Tami has a record.
The record broke.

Write each sentence correctly. Use a capital letter to begin each important word in a proper noun. *pages 162-163*

23. I play on new year's day.
24. We go out on labor day.
25. He plays tennis tuesday.
26. Is halloween in october?

You are going to write a friendly letter. *pages 170-175*

27. Write today's date at the top of the letter.
28. Think of a person you want to write to. Write the person's name in the greeting *Dear* ___ .
29. Write a paragraph of three or four sentences. You might tell about something that happened to you or a place you visited.
30. Write the closing *Your friend.*
31. Write your name.

A Poem

How many ways did you act today? What were you like this morning? Were you as sleepy as a bear in winter? What were you like on the playground today? Were you as quick as the wind?

In just one day, you act in many different ways. You can use different words to tell about all your feelings. Many times you will use words like happy or sad or quiet. Sometimes you will compare yourself to something else. In this poem, the author describes many ways a child like you can feel.

I CAN BE . . .

It's fun to see
What I can be . . .
To imagine a world
That just suits me!

I can be as quiet
as snowflakes
falling to ground.

Or,
I can be as noisy as
the bang balloons make
when they break.

I can be as shy
as a lamb that's
playing hide-and-seek.

Or,
I can be as bold
as a knight
in shining armor.

I can be as calm
and still as
a moonlit night.

Or,
I can be as lively
as a big brass band.

I can be as lazy
as a summer day.

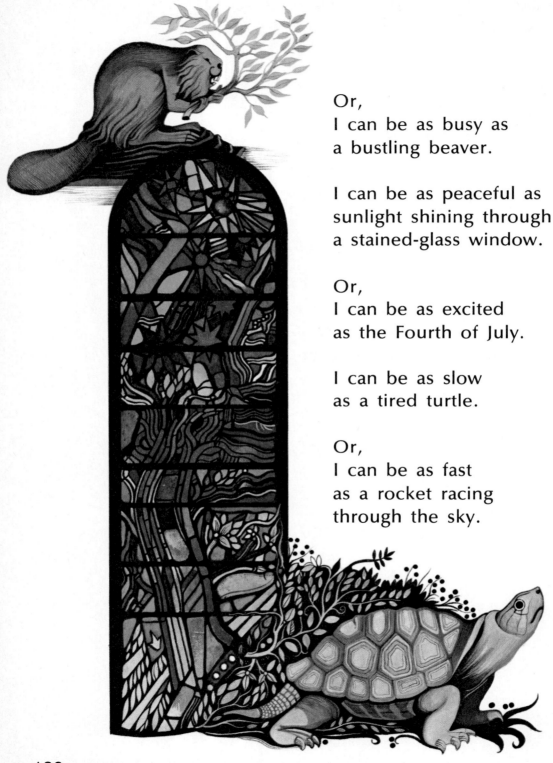

Or,
I can be as busy as
a bustling beaver.

I can be as peaceful as
sunlight shining through
a stained-glass window.

Or,
I can be as excited
as the Fourth of July.

I can be as slow
as a tired turtle.

Or,
I can be as fast
as a rocket racing
through the sky.

I can shout and laugh
Or sit and brood—
And change the world
To fit my mood!
   A. K. Roche

Activities

1. **Creative Writing** Words can be used to describe how you feel. Read this sentence.

  I am as <u>happy</u> as a <u>sunny</u> <u>day</u>.

The word *happy* tells how the person feels. The words *sunny day* help you imagine how the person feels. In the poem "I Can Be . . . ," the author uses words to tell how he feels. He also uses words to help you imagine how he feels. Make a list of all the words in the poem that tell you how the author feels. Next to it, make a list of the words that help you imagine what the author feels. Here is an example.

   quiet snowflakes

2. Draw a picture of something that shows how you feel. Do not draw a picture of yourself. A sunny day is a picture for a happy feeling. Think of a special feeling. Draw a special picture for it.

Grammar and
Related Language Skills

Practical Communication

Creative Expression

Adjectives

Words that name people, places, or things are *nouns*. Sometimes you want to tell more about the nouns. You use special words to describe them.

- Read these sentences.

Donna has a kite.
Donna has a red kite.

The word *kite* is a noun. The word *red* describes the kite. *Red* is an *adjective*.

> An **adjective** is a word that describes a noun.

- Read each pair of sentences. The underlined word in each sentence is a noun.

The <u>boy</u> makes a kite.
The little <u>boy</u> makes a kite.

He uses <u>paper</u>.
He uses brown <u>paper</u>.

The kite has a <u>tail</u>.
The kite has a long <u>tail</u>.

They fly the kite in a <u>field</u>.
They fly the kite in a big <u>field</u>.

The second sentence in each pair has an adjective that tells more about the underlined noun. Find the adjectives.

Talk About It

Read each sentence. Find the adjective. Then find
the noun it describes.

1. I save new stamps.
2. You save old bottles.
3. She saves small coins.

4. We save round rocks.
5. He saves blue shells.
6. They save large postcards.

Skills Practice

Read each sentence. Write the adjective. Then write
the noun it describes.

1. The little girl looked.
2. She lost a green stamp.
3. It fell into a big hole.
4. A big boy found it.
5. A huge dog barked.
6. A white cat ran.

7. We save old stamps.
8. Pat reads a large book.
9. She found a blue stamp.
10. Carl drove a yellow car.
11. A small store sold coins.
12. A man bought a gold coin.

Writing Sentences

Imagine that you save rocks. Write three sentences
about your rocks. Use adjectives in your sentences.
You may use the adjectives in the box.

| round | flat | tiny | red | small | yellow |

Sample Answer 1. little, girl

More About Adjectives

You can use different adjectives to describe a noun. The adjectives in the green box tell how a person, place, or thing *looks*.

red	big	old
orange	little	new
yellow	long	clean
green	short	dirty

- Choose an adjective to complete each sentence. Describe what you see in the picture. The adjectives in the green box may help you.

I have a ___ mouse.
The mouse has a ___ tail.
The mouse lives in a ___ cage.
The mouse eats a ___ piece of cheese.

The words in the orange box are adjectives, too. They tell how a person, place, or thing *feels*.

hot	wet	bumpy
warm	dry	smooth
cold	sticky	hard
cool	sharp	soft

- Choose an adjective from the orange box to complete each sentence.

We found a ___ rock.　　　It fell in the ___ water.
It had a ___ edge.　　　You wrapped it in ___ cloth.

Here are some more adjectives. These adjectives tell how a person, place, or thing *sounds*, *tastes*, or *smells*.

loud	low	sweet
soft	squeaky	sour
high	fresh	salty

- Choose an adjective from the blue box to complete each sentence.

Lisa heard a ___ noise.
She smelled the ___ air.
Jean tasted the ___ berries.

Talk About It

Complete each sentence. Use an adjective. These adjectives will come from all three boxes.

1. I pet the ___ kitten.
2. We fed it ___ milk.
3. We heard the ___ dog.
4. It has a ___ bark.

Skills Practice

Complete each sentence with an adjective. Write the sentence.

1. We hit a ___ ball.
2. He wore a ___ cap.
3. She swung the ___ bat.
4. It was a ___ day.
5. We went to a ___ park.
6. I swam in a ___ pool.
7. You drank ___ water.
8. We ate ___ ice cream.

Writing Sentences

Think about one of these things. Write three sentences telling about it. Use adjectives in your sentences.

1. Something you like
2. Your best friend

Adjectives That Compare

You know that an adjective describes a noun. A *noun* names a person, place, or thing. An *adjective* describes how the noun looks, feels, sounds, smells, or tastes.

Adjectives can also be used to compare nouns. You may have a fast model car. Your friend may have a car that is faster than yours.

● Read these sentences.

Sue found an <u>old</u> stamp.
Tom found an <u>older</u> stamp than Sue did.

In the two sentences the two stamps have been described. One is older than the other. Look at the word *old* in the second sentence. How did it change? To compare two different things, you add *er* to an adjective.

● Now look at these sentences.

Fred saved an <u>old</u> penny.
I saved an <u>older</u> penny than Fred did.
Ruth saved the <u>oldest</u> penny of all.

The three pennies are compared by using the adjectives *old, older,* and *oldest.* How did the word *old* change in the third sentence? To compare several things, add *est* to the adjective.

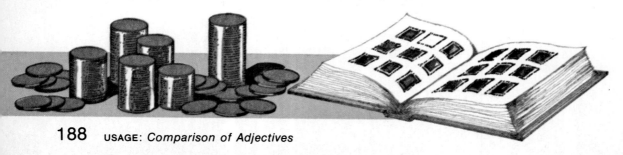

Talk About It

Complete each sentence. Choose the correct
adjective to fill each blank.

1. Ed has a new baseball card.
   I have a ____ card than Ed's.   (newer, newest)
2. Hao built three small model cars.
   The ____ car of all is red.   (smaller, smallest)
3. I bought the ____ airplane in the whole store.
   (longer, longest)
4. Jo has a ____ plane than mine.   (shorter, shortest)
5. Kim has the ____ plane of all.   (shorter, shortest)

Skills Practice

Choose the correct adjective to fill each blank.
Then write the sentence.

1. Jay owns a small football card.
   I own a ____ card than Jay's. (smaller, smallest)
2. Dad owns the ____ card of all.   (smaller, smallest)
3. Eva saved a new bottle cap.
   Don saved a ____ cap than Eva's.   (newer, newest)
4. Pat saved the ____ cap of all.   (newer, newest)
5. May has the ____ dime I have ever seen.
   (older, oldest)
6. Juan kept four clean rocks.
   The ____ rock of all is gray.   (cleaner, cleanest)
7. I found an ____ rock than Kay did.   (older, oldest)

Sample Answer **1.** I own a smaller card than Jay's.

Number Words

Sometimes you want to tell *how many* people, places, or things you are talking about. Then you use number words like *one, two, three.* Number words can be adjectives. They tell *how many.*

● Find the number word in each sentence.

I counted ten birds.
Four birds sat on the fence.
Five birds flew to the tree.
There was one bird on the grass.

Talk About It

Complete each sentence. Use a number word.

1. Rosa made ___ blouses.
2. She put ___ buttons on them.
3. Sam painted ___ pictures.
4. He used ___ colors.

Skills Practice

Complete each sentence with a number word. Write the sentence.

1. Frank baked ___ cookies.
2. Ann made ___ cake.
3. The boys ate ___ eggs.
4. They washed ___ plates.
5. I want ___ pieces.
6. The girls had ___ seeds.
7. They watered ___ plants.
8. They pulled ___ weeds.
9. Pat picked ___ apples.
10. Al made ___ pies.

Articles

You often use the words *a, an,* and *the* before nouns. These three words are called *articles*.

Use *an* before words that begin with vowel sounds.
Use *a* before words that begin with all other sounds.

Jenny flew <u>an</u> airplane.   Brent drove <u>a</u> car.

Use *a* and *an* before singular nouns only.

Use *the* before singular or plural nouns.

Pam sailed <u>the</u> boat.   Ken rode <u>the</u> horses.

Talk About It

Choose a correct article for each sentence.

1. Ben has ___ bicycle.
2. ___ bicycle has a basket.
3. Lynn washes ___ cars.
4. She can drive ___ automobile.

Skills Practice

Complete each sentence. Use a correct article.
Write the sentence.

1. Tim made ___ toy airplane.
2. He used ___ pieces of wood.
3. He carved ___ wood.
4. ___ airplane can fly.

5. Sue bought ___ kites.
6. She runs in ___ park.
7. She eats ___ orange.
8. She saves ___ apple.

Sample Answer 1. Tim made a (the) toy airplane.

Skills Review

Read each sentence. Write the adjective. Then write the noun it describes.

1. The small boy found a rock.
2. He picked up the shiny rock.
3. He put it in a large bag.
4. He collects pretty things.
5. The tall girl has a garden.

Complete each sentence with an adjective. Write the adjective.

6. We walk on the ___ beach.
7. The children like a ___ day.
8. Children play with a ___ ball.
9. They swim in the ___ water.
10. We eat ___ fruit.

Choose the correct adjective to fill each blank. Write the adjective.

11. Joey saw a small bee.
    Rico saw a ___ bee than Joey did.
    (smaller, smallest)
12. Lu saw the ___ bee of all.
    (smaller, smallest)
13. Four large cows came to the barn.
    The ___ cow of all was brown.
    (larger, largest)

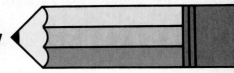

Complete each sentence with a number word. Write
the number word.

14. I counted ____ mice.

15. ____ mice ate cheese.

16. I saw ____ mouse.

17. Tim has ____ papers.

18. He used ____ crayons.

19. He drew ____ pictures.

Complete each sentence. Use a correct article.
Write the article.

20. Cathy has ____ puppet.

21. The puppet wears ____ old dress.

22. ____ dress has two bows.

23. Cathy tied ____ bows.

24. We built ____ doghouse.

Write a story like the one below. Leave blanks for
the adjectives and nouns. Ask a friend for a list of
adjectives and nouns. Do not say why you want
them. Fill in the blanks with the words. See what a
silly story you have written.

The _____ _____ went to the _____.
　　　　adjective　　noun　　　　　　　　noun
　　　　　　　　　　　　　　　　　　　　(place)

A _____ _____ _____ went, too.
　　adjective　　adjective　　noun

They ate _____ _____ for dinner.
　　　　　adjective　　noun
　　　　　(color)　　(plural)

They drank _____ _____ .
　　　　　　adjective　　noun
　　　　　　　　　　　(plural)

Exploring
Language

Words with the Same Meaning

Jeff wrote to thank his uncle for a book.

- Read Jeff's letter.

Thank you for the nice book. It tells a nice story. I like the nice pictures. You are a nice uncle to send it to me.

Jeff used the word *nice* four times. He could have used the words *interesting, wonderful, beautiful,* or *good.* These words are *synonyms* for *nice.*

A **synonym** is a word that has nearly the same meaning as another word.

Talk About It

Read each adjective in the first column. Then find a synonym for it in the second column.

1. big   a. sad
2. noisy   b. lovely
3. pretty   c. loud
4. unhappy   d. large

Skills Practice

Use a synonym for the underlined word. Write your new sentence. You may use the words in the list above.

1. Jan has a <u>pretty</u> hat.
2. She saw a <u>big</u> feather.
3. A <u>smart</u> man sold it.
4. An <u>unhappy</u> boy fell.
5. He lost a <u>bright</u> coin.
6. A <u>noisy</u> horn honked.

Words With Opposite Meanings

● Read these pairs of sentences.

Jill has <u>long</u> hair.   The <u>clean</u> dog is Tag.
Bill has <u>short</u> hair.   The <u>dirty</u> dog is Rags.

The underlined words in each pair of sentences have opposite meanings. These words are *antonyms*.

An **antonym** is a word that means
the opposite of another word.

● Find the antonyms in each pair of sentences.

I drank some hot milk.   Dan has an empty glass.
You drank some cold milk.   Anita has a full glass.

Talk About It

Read each adjective in the first column. Then find an antonym for it in the second column.

1. dry   **a.** closed
2. hard   **b.** bottom
3. big   **c.** wet
4. open   **d.** soft
5. top   **e.** small

Skills Practice

Use an antonym for each underlined word. Write your new sentence. You may use the words from above.

1. I have a <u>big</u> jar.   **3.** It had <u>hard</u> clay in it.
2. Pat put it on a <u>top</u> shelf. **4.** I keep it in a <u>dry</u> place.

Making Adjectives

Some words are made by adding an ending to another word. Many adjectives are made by adding *y* to certain nouns.

> bump
> bump**y**
> We drove on a *bumpy* road.

The spelling of some words changes before you add *y*.

> sun
> sun**ny**
> It is a *sunny* day.

If a word ends with consonant, vowel, consonant, double the last consonant and add **y** to form the adjective.

● Make each word an adjective.

rain   mud   dust

● Read each sentence. Find the adjective.

We played indoors on that rainy afternoon.
The baby stepped in the muddy water.
I wiped the dusty table.

Talk About It

Make the word that comes after each sentence into an adjective. Use the adjective to complete the sentence.

1. I live on a ____ street.   (hill)
2. This is a ____ beach.   (sand)
3. We walked on a ____ path.   (rock)
4. It is a ____ morning.   (sun)

Skills Practice

Make the word in ( ) into an adjective.
Complete the sentence with the adjective.
Write the sentence.

1. We had ____ fish for dinner.   (salt)
2. I washed the ____ dishes.   (dirt)
3. I put my ____ hands in the water.   (soap)
4. They wiped the ____ glasses.   (spot)
5. The ____ dog barked.   (hair)
6. The ____ girl made me laugh.   (fun)
7. You have ____ shoes.   (mud)
8. The ____ boy went to bed.   (sleep)

Writing Sentences

Make each word an adjective. Then write two sentences to describe something. Use the adjectives in your sentences.

1. stick   **2.** fur

Sample Answer 1. We had salty fish for dinner.

Words That Sound the Same

When you write sentences, you need to spell words the right way. Sometimes two words sound the same. But they may not mean the same thing.

- Read these sentences out loud. How are the underlined words the same? How are they different?

I have a pet monkey.
The monkey has one blue <u>eye</u>.

Words like <u>I</u> and <u>eye</u> sound the same. They are not spelled the same. They do not have the same meaning.

- Read each pair of sentences. How are the underlined words the same? Spell each underlined word. Tell its meaning.

I <u>see</u> the ship.
The ship sails on the <u>sea</u>.

The water was <u>blue</u>.
The wind <u>blew</u> hard.

Do you <u>know</u> a sailor?
<u>No</u>, I never met one.

The <u>sail</u> was torn.
They took it to a <u>sale</u>.

Sailors <u>write</u> home often.
He was <u>right</u> about the storm.

Do you <u>hear</u> the wind?
It is calm <u>here</u> now.

The sailors have <u>two</u> ships.
They want <u>to</u> buy another one.
They have a rowboat, <u>too</u>.

Talk About It

Use the correct word in each sentence. Give a
reason for your answer.

1. I like the ___ dress. (blew, blue)
2. Did you ___ it? (see, sea)
3. It is on ___ in the store. (sail, sale)
4. I want ___ buy it. (two, to, too)

Skills Practice

Choose the word with the correct meaning for each
sentence. Write the sentence.

1. Do you ___ about the new pet store? (no, know)
2. It is near ___ . (hear, here)
3. The fish are on ___ . (sail, sale)
4. One fish has a green ___ . (eye, I)
5. They come from the deep ___ . (sea, see)
6. I have ___ money. (no, know)
7. Do you want ___ dollars? (two, to, too)
8. Can ___ buy the fish now? (eye, I)

Writing Sentences

Pretend you work in a library. Write a sentence
using each word.

1. two   **3.** to
2. blue   **4.** hear

Sample Answer 1. Do you know about the new pet store?

Skills Review

Read each sentence. Write a synonym for the underlined word. The words in the box may help you.

large	tiny
pretty	friendly
noisy	wonderful

1. You like <u>loud</u> music.
2. I have a <u>big</u> box of records.
3. A <u>nice</u> girl gave them to me.
4. I play a <u>lovely</u> song.
5. It tells a <u>good</u> story.
6. The record has a <u>small</u> scratch.

Read each sentence. Write an antonym for the underlined word. The words in the box may help you.

7. We baked a <u>big</u> cake.
8. I used a <u>new</u> mix.
9. You washed the <u>empty</u> bowl.
10. You put the <u>dry</u> bowl away.
11. I washed the <u>dirty</u> sponge.
12. We are <u>fast</u> workers.
13. We used a <u>strong</u> pan.
14. It was on a <u>high</u> shelf.

clean	small
slow	wet
old	full
low	weak

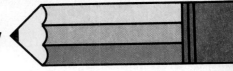

Make the word in ( ) into an adjective. Complete the sentence with the adjective. Write the adjective.

15. I laughed at the ___ monkey. (hair)
16. He made a ___ face. (fun)
17. We went to a ___ beach. (sand)
18. It was a ___ day. (sun)
19. We drove on a ___ road. (dust)

Choose the word with the correct meaning for each sentence. Write the word.

20. I have ___ gloves. (to, two, too)
21. I wear them ___ keep warm. (to, two, too)
22. I bought them on ___ . (sail, sale)
23. The gloves are ___ . (blew, blue)
24. The store has ___ more gloves. (know, no)
25. Can ___ wear them tonight? (I, eye)

Copy the words below on a sheet of paper. Draw a line from each word at the left to its antonym. The antonyms are listed at the right. The first one is done for you.

stop	late
early	hate
open	go
love	cry
laugh	shut

Exploring Language

Taking Notes

You often read books for a special reason. Sometimes you need to gather facts for a report.

It is hard to remember all the important facts after you finish reading. You can help yourself remember important facts by taking notes. When you *take notes,* you write down all the important facts.

Andy has to write a report about what a painter must do before she begins to paint. He read this paragraph.

A painter must do many things before she starts her work. First she decides what she wants to paint. She may want to paint a picture of some flowers. Then she must decide what colors she will use. The colors will add to her painting. Finally she gathers her paints and brushes together.

Andy took these notes as he read the paragraph.

1. A painter must do many things before she begins to paint.
2. She decides what she wants to paint.
3. She decides what colors she will use.
4. She gathers her paints and brushes together.

• Read Andy's notes again. All his notes tell what a painter must do before she begins painting. Notice that all his notes are complete sentences.

Talk About It

Read this paragraph.

> Dance is beautiful to watch. Dancers must train for many years. Many start when they are very young. Dancers must go to special schools. They spend a lot of time learning and practicing dance.

Pretend you have to write a report about training to be a dancer. Which of these notes would you take?

1. Dance is beautiful.
2. Dancers train for many years.
3. They go to special schools.
4. They spend much time learning and practicing dance.

Skills Practice

Read this paragraph.

> Pedro was going to be in a play. First he had to try out for a part. Then he had to learn the part. He and his sister went over it many times. Now everyone in the play has to practice together.

Pretend you have to write a report telling about Pedro's part in a play. Write the notes you would take.

1. Pedro had to try out for a part.
2. He had to learn the part.
3. His sister helped him learn his part.
4. Everyone in the play has to practice together.

Organizing Notes

When you give a report, you want to make sure everyone understands your ideas. You must put your facts in an order that makes sense. First you read to find the important facts. Then you take notes. Read your notes carefully.

● Look at Jane's notes.

> 1. Many forests catch on fire every year.
> 2. People cause most forest fires.
> 3. Dry summers can cause some forest fires, too.
> 4. Special fire fighters put out forest fires.

Jane's notes are in a good order. She numbered her notes in the order she will write them in her report. She will use her first note for her main idea sentence. She will use the other notes for her detail sentences. The facts in her paragraph will have the same order as the facts in her notes.

Talk About It

Read these notes. Put them in an order that makes sense.

1. It belongs to a family of stars.
2. The sun is really a star.
3. We call this family the *Milky Way.*
4. There are many other families of stars.

Skills Practice

Read these notes. Write them in an order that makes sense.

1. It started out as dust and hot gas.
2. The earth is very old.
3. The dust and gas were left over from the sun.
4. At last it began to look like it does now.
5. Slowly the earth changed.

Write these notes in an order that makes sense.

1. At first people tried to copy birds.
2. At last someone made an airplane.
3. People always wanted to fly.
4. Next people tried to copy kites.

Stories

Thinking About Stories

Do you like to hear and to read stories? You can read stories in books. You can watch them on TV. In a good story you want to know what happened. You cannot stop reading or listening until you find out.

Most stories have three parts. The parts are called the *beginning,* the *middle,* and the *end.* The beginning of the story uses sentences that tell who or what the story is about. Some sentences also tell when and where the story happens. The sentences in the middle tell what happened to people or things in the story. The sentences in the end tell how everything works out in the story.

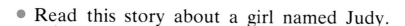

● Read this story about a girl named Judy.

Judy was sleeping one night. She heard strange noises downstairs. They sounded like someone was knocking things over. Judy was very scared. She woke her parents. Her mother called the police. Everyone looked around the house. To their surprise, they found the noise was made by Judy's dog. He was playing with his bone.

The story about Judy has a beginning, a middle, and an end. The beginning tells that the story is about Judy. It also tells when and where the story happened. The middle tells the problem that Judy had. The end tells how the problem was solved.

Talking About Stories

Read the story on the other page.

1. Which sentences tell what happened at the beginning of the story?

2. Which sentences tell what happened in the middle of the story?

3. Which sentences tell what happened at the end of the story?

4. Think of another ending for the story. What would it be?

A Class Story

Thinking About Stories

Your class is going to write a story together. Your story should have a beginning, a middle, and an end. Your story will be about a spaceship that lands outside your school. The picture below may help you think of sentences to write for each part of your story. Talk about what you want to happen in the beginning and middle of your story. How will your story end?

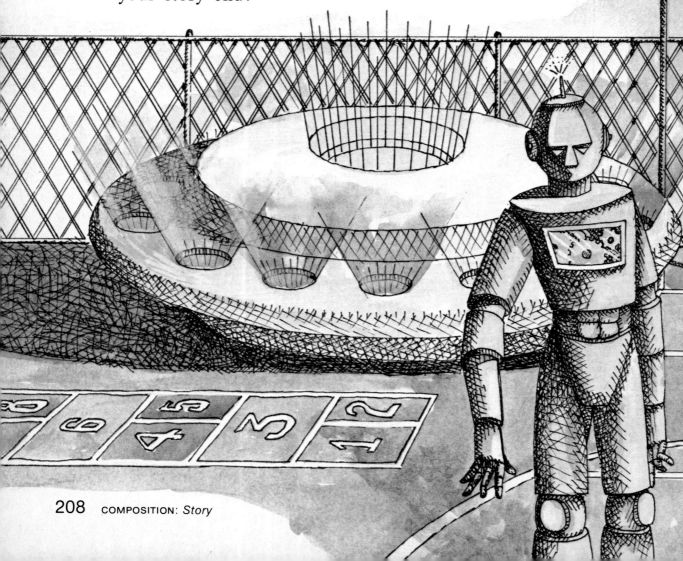

Writing a Story

Your teacher will write the story on the board.

1. You may begin your story with these two sentences: *One morning we were sitting in class. Suddenly we heard a loud noise outside.*

2. Now you are ready to write the middle of your story. Think of one or two sentences that describe the spaceship that landed. Think of one or two sentences that tell about the space people who step out.

3. Reread the middle part. Did you choose adjectives that really help you see the spaceship and the space people?

4. Now write the end of your story. Think of one or two sentences that tell what happened to the space people and the spaceship. You might tell what your class did.

5. Reread your whole story together. Does it have an interesting middle and end? You may want to write the story and draw your own pictures to go with it.

Your Own Story

Thinking About Your Story

Now you are going to write your own story. You may want to write a story of your own or you may want to use the ideas that follow. Pretend that someone named Ray went to the zoo. Something interesting happened to him there.

Remember your story must have a beginning, a middle, and an end. Look at the pictures below. They will help you write the sentences for the middle of your story. The Word Bank shows some words you can use in your sentences.

Writing Your Story

1. Begin your story with these two sentences:
   Ray went to the zoo. He visited the monkeys.

2. Now you are ready to write the middle of your story. Look at the two pictures. Write one or two sentences that tell what Ray did when he visited the monkeys. Next write one or two sentences that tell what the monkey did with Ray's cap.

3. You can now write the end of your story. What could happen to Ray and the monkey? Did Ray get his cap back? How did he get it back? Write one or two sentences for the end of your story.

Word Bank

red
cap
visited
peanuts
fed
grabbed
yelled
zookeeper
laughed
funny

Edit Your Story

Now read your story carefully. Answer these questions as you read.

1. Does your story have a beginning, middle, and end?

2. Do your sentences tell clearly what happened in each part of the story?

3. What adjectives did you use in your sentences?

4. Did you use capital letters and periods where they are needed? Did you indent the first word?

5. Did you spell the words correctly? Use the Word Bank to help you.

Correct your mistakes. Make a good copy of your story. You may want to read your story to the class.

Checking Skills

Write each adjective. Then write the noun it describes.   *pages 184-184*

1. Kevin has clean paper.
2. He found a red pen.

3. He drew a little clown.
4. The clown had big ears.

Write an adjective to complete each sentence.   *pages 186-187*

5. The ___ snow fell fast.
6. She wore ___ mittens.

7. I made a ___ snowball.
8. He drank some ___ milk.

Write the correct adjective to fill each blank.   *pages 188-189*

9. Joe wore a warm hat.
   Judy wore a ___ hat than Joe's.   (warmest, warmer)
10. Ellie wore the ___ hat of all.   (warmest, warmer)

Write a number word to complete each sentence.   *page 190*

11. I have ___ stamps.
12. I buy ___ book.

13. Kim owns ___ coins.
14. She finds ___ jars.

Complete each sentence. Write the article.   *page 191*

15. Tim flies ___ airplane.
16. It is only ___ toy.

17. Tim went to ___ airport.
18. He saw ___ real airplane.

Write a synonym for the underlined word.   *page 194*

| large | good | shiny | lovely |

19. Cathy made a <u>pretty</u> bowl.
20. She used <u>bright</u> colors.

21. I found some <u>big</u> flowers.
22. A <u>nice</u> woman bought it.

Write an antonym for the underlined word. *page 195*

big	closed	bottom	dry

23. I saw an <u>open</u> door.
24. A <u>little</u> boy ran out.

25. He sat on the <u>top</u> step.
26. The boy had a <u>wet</u> towel.

Write the word with the correct meaning for each sentence.
pages 198-199

27. My school is near ____ . (here, hear)
28. I have gone there for ____ years. (to, two, too)

Read these sentences from a story. Think about the
right order for the sentences. *pages 206-211*

29. **a.** He was afraid to come down.
   b. She called the fire station.
   c. One morning Mops ran up a tall tree.
   d. Angela owned a pet monkey named Mops.
   e. A fire fighter climbed up and saved Mops.
   f. Angela could not reach him.
   g. Mops liked to climb trees.

Now put the sentences in order.

30. First, write the sentences that tell who, when,
   and where at the beginning of the story.
31. Next, write the sentences that tell about the
   problem in the middle of the story.
32. Last, write the sentences that tell how the
   problem was solved at the end of the story.

A Story

Have you ever thought of exploring a new place? Suppose you got lost along the way. What would you do? In this story, a young boy and his horse travel along an old trail. Follow the characters and share their adventure with them.

Blaze Finds the Trail

One day Billy's mother made some sandwiches for him, because he and Blaze were going for a very long ride. They were going to explore an old road through the woods that no one ever used any more. This was exciting. Blaze seemed to enjoy the ride as much as Billy.

They came to the place where the old road turned off, straight into the deep woods. Although it was overgrown with grass and weeds, Billy could still see the deep ruts wagons had made in the ground many years ago. He wanted to see where they would take them.

They came to a place where a dead tree was leaning across the road. There was barely room for Blaze to go under it. Billy had to lie flat on Blaze's back, and they just squeezed through.

Then they came to a fallen tree across the road, but Blaze was a fine jumper and sailed over it easily.

They had gone a long way, when Billy saw another big tree across the path. The branches held it up, so that it was too high to jump and too low to go under.

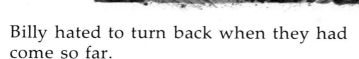

Billy hated to turn back when they had come so far.

"Let's try to go around it, Blaze," said Billy. "There must be some way to do it."

The woods were very thick, and each time they tried to get back to the path there were fallen trees or thick woods in the way. They were getting farther and farther from the old road, and still they could not find any opening.

At last they were able to turn back toward the road. Now Billy felt that everything was going to be all right. But they had not gone far before they came to a very deep gully. Billy's heart sank, for he knew they could never get down such a place. They would have to go back again and try a different way. Billy had to lead his pony, for the woods were too thick for him to ride.

There was nothing in sight but woods, and Billy began to be worried. Which way was the road? When he looked for the sun to find what direction he should go, he saw that the sky had become very dark and stormy. It looked very strange, and he was frightened. They must get home before the storm.

It was growing very dark and still they could find no sign of a road. Billy was tired and frightened. He knew they were lost. He sat down to rest. Blaze rubbed his soft nose against Billy as if to say, "Don't worry, I'll take care of you." But now a strong wind was blowing, and the sky was very dark.

When Billy got up, Blaze started off pulling Billy with him. He seemed to know just where he wanted to go, so Billy followed him.

"Do you really know the way, Blaze?" he cried. "If you only get us out of these woods, I'll give you carrots and sugar every day. Lots and lots of them."

Blaze went right on, dodging around rocks and trees, but always going the same direction.

Suddenly, through the bushes, Billy saw something that made him very happy. It was only an old stone wall, but now he knew they were on the right track. His father had often told how the early settlers had built these walls, with stones they cleared from the land. And where there were walls, there had once been fields and roads leading to them.

Then just ahead he saw an opening in the wall, and a path leading ahead.

"You are wonderful, Blaze!" he cried. "You've found the way."

Now at last he could get in the saddle again, and they could go faster. The wind was growing stronger, and he knew the woods were no place to be in a storm.

They went at a gallop, for the wind was roaring through the treetops and the sky was very black. Suddenly they heard a loud crack, and Blaze leaped forward just as a big dead tree crashed down in the path behind them. "This must be another hurricane." Billy shouted to Blaze. "We'll have to race."

Blaze was galloping as hard as he could, and Billy was dodging the low branches when he saw, just ahead of them, a wide road. Nothing had ever looked so wonderful to him. Now he knew that home was just a mile down the road.

"You did it!" Billy shouted in Blaze's ear as the wind howled around them. "You're a wonderful pony!"

—*C. W. Anderson*

Activities

1. **Creative Writing**   Open any book and look on the page until you find the name of a person, such as "doctor." Then look for the name of a place, such as "field." Then find the name of an object, such as "tire." Write a story involving the three words you have selected. For example, your story might tell about a doctor with a tire in a field. Think of some problem that the person must solve in the story.

2. Look in the library for other books about Blaze and Billy by C. W. Anderson. Read them and share the adventures with your class.

Grammar and Related Language Skills

Review of Verbs in the Present and Past
Verbs in the Future
Helping Verbs
Contractions

Practical Communication

Using the Library
Writing a Report

Creative Expression

A True Story

Verbs in the Present and Past

Verbs are very important words in sentences. A *verb* is a word that names an action. It is in the predicate part of a sentence. The *predicate part* of a sentence tells what action the subject part does. Words like *run*, *jump*, and *climb* are verbs.

Ted <u>buys</u> a fishing pole.   Shelly <u>finds</u> a sleeping bag.

Verbs name actions. They also tell when the action happens. When you talk about things that happen now, you use a *verb in the present*.

A **verb in the present** names an action that happens now.

When you talk about things that happened before, you use a *verb in the past*.

A **verb in the past** names an action that happened before.

Mr. Peck <u>talked</u> to our class. He <u>showed</u> us some maps.

Add **s** to most verbs in the present when they work with singular nouns. Jane <u>swims</u> in the pool.

If a verb ends in *s*, *ss*, *ch*, *sh*, or *x*, add **es** to make the verb work with a singular noun. Mr. Peck <u>teaches</u> school.

Use the correct verb in the present.

1. Helen ____ to school.   (rush)
2. The children ____ in the yard.   (play)
3. Mike ____ his friend.   (see)

Use the correct verb in the past.

4. Susan ____ unusual stamps.   (save)
5. She ____ the stamps in a book.   (place)
6. Her sister ____ the book to school.   (carry)
7. I ____ the stamps yesterday.   (study)

Skills Practice _____

Use the correct verb in the present. Write the sentence.

1. Chris ____ a model sailboat.   (build)
2. She ____ for strong wood.   (search)
3. Tod ____ the new sailboat in the lake.   (try)
4. He ____ the broken sail.   (fix)
5. They ____ the sailboat in a race.   (enter)

Use the correct verb in the past. Write the sentence.

6. I ____ in the woods last week.   (walk)
7. We ____ along the trails.   (move)
8. Barbara ____ the tent.   (carry)
9. Uncle Ray ____ in the lake.   (fish)
10. Tommy ____ the eggs.   (fry)
11. He ____ the new frying pan.   (try)

Sample Answers **1.** Chris builds a model sailboat. **6.** I walked in the woods last week.

Verbs in the Future

You know that verbs can tell about things that happen now. Verbs can tell about things that already happened. Verbs can also tell about things that will happen in the future.

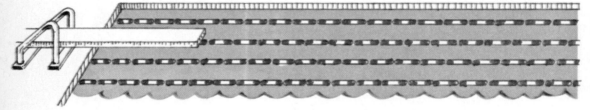

● Look at the verbs in these sentences.

Luis <u>swims</u> in the pool.   He <u>learned</u> to dive yesterday.

The verb *swims* names an action that happens in the present time. The verb *learned* names an action that happened in the past.

● Now read this sentence.

Luis <u>will swim</u> in a race next week.   He <u>will try</u> to win.

The verbs *will swim* and *will try* name actions that will happen at a future time.

> The **future tense of a verb** names an action that will take place in the future.

Verbs that show action in the future have a main verb and the helping verb *will* or *shall*.

> A **helping verb** is a verb that helps the main verb to name an action.

Talk About It

Find the verb in each sentence. Tell whether the verb names an action in the present, the past, or the future.

1. Linda Campos will swim in the race next Tuesday.
2. Her sister raced on our team last week.
3. The whole Campos family likes sports.
4. Mr. Campos will watch the races all day.
5. Mrs. Campos swims on a team also.
6. She liked the water when she was very young.

Skills Practice

Write each verb. Then write whether each verb is in the present, the past, or the future.

1. Tommy O'Brien plays baseball.
2. He played baseball with his team this morning.
3. They will play again tomorrow morning.
4. Our town will have another baseball team soon.
5. Their shirts will be red.
6. I like football better than baseball.
7. My father watched my game last week.
8. He yelled very loudly.
9. My team uses the school football field.
10. We want to win all our games.

Sample Answer 1. plays, present

Using Verbs in the Past

You know that a verb in the past names an action that happened before. You add *ed* to most verbs to name an action in the past. Some verbs do not follow the usual rule. Sometimes the whole word changes.

Here are some verbs that change to name an action in the past.

VERB	VERB IN THE PAST
go	went
see	saw
do	did
eat	ate
know	knew
fly	flew
give	gave
grow	grew
take	took
begin	began

● Read each sentence. Notice the verb that names an action in the past.

We <u>went</u> to the game.
A player <u>saw</u> the ball.
Our team <u>did</u> very well.
We <u>ate</u> some peanuts.
We <u>knew</u> many people

The ball <u>flew</u> up high.
We all <u>gave</u> a cheer.
Our hopes <u>grew</u> higher.
One player <u>took</u> his turn.
The band <u>began</u> to play.

Talk About It

Complete each sentence. Use a verb that names an action in the past.

1. Our class ___ to the race. (go)
2. A girl ___ the finish line. (see)
3. What ___ she do? (do)
4. We ___ hot dogs after the race. (eat)

Skills Practice

Read each sentence. Write each sentence with the verb that names an action in the past.

1. I ___ to the park. (go)
2. Many trees ___ there. (grow)
3. A boy ___ an apple to his friend. (give)
4. He ___ a handstand. (do)
5. He ___ he would fall. (know)
6. Two girls ___ turns swinging. (take)
7. Two birds ___ from the tree. (fly)
8. A boy ___ a race. (begin)

Writing Sentences

Pretend your class took a trip yesterday.

1. Write a sentence to tell where you *went.*
2. Write a sentence to tell what you *saw.*
3. Write a sentence to tell what you *did.*

Sample Answer 1. I went to the park.

Helping Verbs

Sometimes verbs need help to name an action in the past. The words *have* and *has* can be helping verbs.

- Read these sentences.

> Barbara <u>has</u> <u>played</u> well with our team.
> We <u>have</u> <u>practiced</u> all day.

The words *has* and *have* help the verbs to name an action.

A **helping verb** is a word that helps a verb to name an action.

- Look at the sentences in the box again. When you use a helping verb with a verb, the form of the verb changes.

Add **ed** to most verbs when you use them with the helping verb *have* or *has.*

- Read each sentence. What is the verb? What is the helping verb?

The game has started.
She has jumped very high.
They have scored two points.
The players have walked out of the gym.

Mimi Forsyth, Monkmeyer Press Photo Service

Talk About It

Complete each sentence with the correct form of verb.

1. Bob has ____ the game. (start)
2. Sue has ____ the ball. (kick)
3. They have ____ for a long time. (play)
4. We have ____ the team. (join)
5. Cory has ____ to first base. (walk)

Skills Practice

Read each sentence. Write the helping verb and the verb.

1. Mindy has wanted a new ball.
2. She has earned some money.
3. I have listed our names.
4. We have started a new game.

Write each sentence using the correct form of the verb.

5. We have ____ tennis everyday. (play)
6. Ted has ____ a lot. (learn)
7. He has ____ me for my help. (thank)
8. I have ____ the games. (enjoy)
9. Jane has ____ to our town. (move)
10. She has ____ schools. (change)
11. We have ____ to her. (talk)
12. She has ____ basketball. (play)
13. We have ____ a good player. (need)

Sample Answers **1.** has wanted **5.** We have played tennis everyday.

More Verbs in the Past

Remember that some verbs do not add *ed* to name an action in the past. The verbs *go, see, do,* and *eat* change completely. These verbs change again when they are used with *have* or *has*.

VERB	PAST WITH HAVE OR HAS
go	have or has gone
see	have or has seen
do	have or has done
eat	have or has eaten
know	have or has known
fly	have or has flown
give	have or has given
grow	have or has grown
take	have or has taken
begin	have or has begun

- Read each sentence. Find the verb and helping verb.

My sister has gone out.
I have seen her run.
She has done her best.
She has eaten well.
We have known for a week.

She has flown to the city.
We have given her a prize.
Her score has grown.
She has taken first place.
Her race has begun.

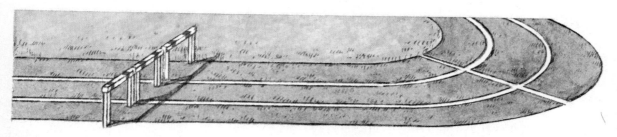

Talk About It

Tell the correct form of the verb.

1. Some children have ___ to the barn. (go)
2. They have ___ a lot of work there. (do)
3. A girl has ___ a little pony. (see)
4. The pony has ___ some hay. (eat)

Skills Practice

Read each sentence. Write the helping verb and the verb.

1. We have gone to a race.
2. I have seen the winner.
3. She has done a good job.
4. He has eaten a good meal.

Write each sentence using the correct form of the verb.

5. Pat has ___ what he had to do. (know)
6. He has ___ through his work. (fly)
7. The children have ___ him their help. (give)
8. Pat's score has ___ higher. (grow)
9. We have ___ a picnic lunch to the game. (take)
10. It has ___ to rain. (begin)

Writing Sentences

Pretend you have gone to a ball game.

1. Write a sentence to tell where you *have gone*.
2. Write a sentence to tell what you *have seen*.
3. Write a sentence to tell what you *have done* there.

Sample Answers 1. have gone 5. Pat has known what he had to do.

USAGE: *Irregular Past Participle* 229

Skills Review

Use the correct verb in the present. Write the verb.

1. A bird ___ for food.   (search)
2. It ___ through the clouds.   (fly)
3. The bird ___ insects in the grass.   (catch)

Use the correct verb in the past. Write the verb.

4. The cat ___ up a tree.   (race)
5. Sally ___ everywhere.   (look)
6. The baby ___ about the lost cat.   (cry)

Write each verb. Then write whether the verb is in the present, the past, or the future.

7. The cat slept.   **9.** The bird sings loudly.
8. The dog will bark.   **10.** Pilar will laugh.

Write the verb that names an action in the past.

11. He ___ to the football game.   (go)
12. We ___ two boxes of popcorn.   (eat)
13. She ___ the touchdown.   (see)

Write the helping verb and the verb.

14. You have played tennis.   **16.** She has raced ahead.
15. He has practiced hard.   **17.** I have tossed the ball.

Write the correct form of the verb.

18. Diane has ___ the most points.   (score)
19. Mike has ___ the highest.   (jump)
20. They have ___ very well.   (play)
21. We have ___ in first place.   (finish)

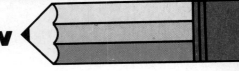
Write the helping verb and the verb.

22. I have gone to the schoolyard.
23. She has eaten lunch.
24. We have done this every afternoon.
25. He has seen them often.

Write the correct form of the verb.

26. She has ____ a new fishing rod for Tim.   (see)
27. We have ____ to buy it.   (go)
28. Tim has ____ us to the store.   (take)
29. He has ____ dinner with us.   (eat)
30. Sue has ____ her model airplane.   (fly)
31. She has ____ to build model airplanes.   (begin)

Write these verbs on cards.

| go | see | do | eat |

Write these two helping verbs on cards.

| have | has |

Match a helping verb card with a verb card. Does the form of the verb change? Spell the correct verb form.

Exploring Language

Contractions

Sometimes you use short cuts when you write. Some words can be joined together to make a shorter word that means the same thing.

can not	do not	does not
can't	don't	doesn't
did not	have not	has not
didn't	haven't	hasn't

A **contraction** is a word made up of two words. The words are joined together to make one word. One or more letters are left out.

Use an **apostrophe** in a contraction to take the place of the letter or letters that are left out.

● Read each pair of sentences. Find the contraction. What words make up each contraction?

I can not swim very well.
I can't swim very well.

I did not bring my bathing suit.
I didn't bring my bathing suit.

He does not own a boat.
He doesn't own a boat.

We have not found the lake.
We haven't found the lake.

Talk About It

Read each sentence using a contraction for the underlined words. Spell the contraction.

1. Our player <u>does not</u> have the ball.
2. He <u>has not</u> scored a point.
3. We <u>can not</u> stop the other team.
4. Our fans <u>do not</u> look happy.
5. We <u>have not</u> lost yet.
6. They <u>did not</u> blow the whistle.

Skills Practice

Write each sentence using a contraction for the underlined words.

1. Max <u>can not</u> catch the ball.
2. Molly <u>does not</u> have a glove.
3. The team <u>has not</u> found a coach.
4. My friends <u>have not</u> come.
5. They <u>do not</u> like basketball.
6. We <u>did not</u> play well.
7. We <u>can not</u> find an empty space.

Writing Sentences

Write a sentence about each of these. Use a contraction.

1. Something you can not do
2. Something you do not like to do

Sample Answer 1. Max can't catch the ball.

Prefixes

Some words are formed by adding a letter or letters to the beginning of other words.

A **prefix** is a group of letters added to the beginning of a word.

The prefix *un* can mean *the opposite of.*

Barry <u>hooked</u> the gate.

A visitor <u>unhooked</u> it.

We <u>lock</u> the door each night.

We <u>unlock</u> it in the morning.

The prefix *re* often means *again.*

Ms. Parker <u>filled</u> her plate.
Later she <u>refilled</u> it.

Mr. Kane <u>built</u> a doghouse.
He <u>rebuilt</u> it a year later.

- Read each pair of sentences.

Joan tied her shoes.
She untied them at bedtime.

Larry read the story.
He reread it for his friend.

Look at the verbs. What prefix was added in the second sentence of each pair? How does the prefix change the meaning of the verb?

Talk About It

Add the prefix *un* to each verb to make a new verb. What does the new verb mean?

1. cover   **2.** snap   **3.** do

Add the prefix *re* to each verb to make a new verb. What does the new verb mean?

4. paint   **5.** write   **6.** visit

Skills Practice

Add the prefix *un* to each underlined verb. Write the second sentence with the new verb.

1. Brady <u>buttons</u> his coat.
He _____ it on warm days.

2. Bea <u>snapped</u> her boots.
One boot came _____.

3. I <u>zip</u> my coat outdoors.
I _____ it indoors.

4. We <u>packed</u> the box.
They _____ it.

Add the prefix *re* to each underlined verb. Write the second sentence with the new verb.

5. Mother <u>told</u> a story.
She _____ it many times.

6. Father <u>opened</u> the door.
He _____ it for my sister.

7. I <u>packed</u> a bag.
I _____ it at the motel.

8. Alice <u>played</u> the record.
She _____ it later.

Writing Sentences

Write one sentence using each of the following verbs: *untie, unlock, reopen, reshovel.*

Sample Answers **1.** He unbuttons it on warm days. **5.** She retold it many times.

Different Ways to Say Something

You talk to your friends in certain ways. You often use different words when you talk to your teacher.

- Read the sentences below each picture.

Hey, Jack!

Excuse me, Mrs. Walters.

What's happening?

How are you?

You do not always act the same way. You say things in different ways at different times. When you speak, you often use words you would not use when you write.

Talk About It _____

Pretend that you want to buy something in a store. Which group of words would you say to the store owner?

1. This is a neat bike.
   I like this bike very much.

2. This one is far out, too.
   I really like this one, too.

3. Look at this one.
   Get a load of this!

4. I'll give you a buzz when I've decided.
   I'll give you a call when I've decided.

5. Thank you very much.
   Thanks a bunch.

Pretend you are talking to the team coach in your school. Which group of words would you say?

6. I'm nuts about basketball.
   I enjoy basketball a lot.

7. I can run like crazy.
   I can run very fast.

8. How come I can't join the team?
   Why can't I join the team?

9. I understand.
   I got it.

Skills Review

Read each sentence using a contraction. Write the contraction.

1. I do not fish very often.
2. He has not brought enough worms.
3. We can not find the new hooks.
4. They did not know about the lake.
5. She does not have a fishing rod.
6. We have not caught any fish.
7. I can not ride a bicycle.
8. Robin does not have one.
9. We do not ride very often.
10. You have not found a good hill.
11. Carl has not bought a new bicycle.
12. They did not fix the wheel.

Read the first sentence in each pair. Add the prefix *un* to the underlined verb. Write the new verb that will complete the second sentence.

13. He <u>covers</u> the bird cage at night.
    He ____ it in the morning.

14. I always <u>lock</u> the car door.
    I will ____ it now.

15. The woman <u>tied</u> my packages together.
    I ____ them when I got home.

16. Fay <u>wrapped</u> a gift for Pedro.
    Pedro ____ it at his birthday party.

Read the first sentence in each pair. Add the prefix *re* to the underlined verb. Write the new verb that will complete the second sentence.

17. We <u>painted</u> the house two years ago.
Father ___ it this year.

18. I <u>wrote</u> a story.
I ___ it on clean paper.

19. She <u>packed</u> her suitcase.
She ___ it after her trip.

20. He <u>counted</u> the number of children on the bus.
He ___ when the children got off the bus.

People usually use contractions when they talk to each other. A contraction takes less time to say than the two words that make up the contraction.

Listen to two friends talking to each other. Make a list of the contractions they use. Next to each word, write the two words that make up the contractions.

Exploring
Language

Books of Information

Your school books tell you facts about many different things. Sometimes you need to find facts that you cannot find in your school books.

The library has books called reference books. *Reference books* give facts about many different subjects. They are very helpful when you do reports. The *dictionary* is a reference book. The *encyclopedia* and *atlas* are other reference books you can find in the library.

An *encyclopedia* is a set of books that gives facts about many things. The books are arranged in alphabetical order. You can find out about famous people. You can find information about different countries. You can learn about how people in other parts of the world live. Encyclopedias also give information about the latest discoveries in science. These are only some of the things you can find in an encyclopedia. It has information about almost everything.

An *atlas* is a book of maps. You can find maps of different countries in an atlas. Most atlases have an index to help you find the maps.

Talk About It

Name the reference book you would use to find out about each of these.

1. George Washington
2. A map of France
3. How the people in China live
4. The meaning of the word *humor*

Skills Practice

Name the reference book you would use to find out about each of these. Write **encyclopedia**, **dictionary**, or **atlas**.

1. The meaning of the word *cycle*
2. How skyscrapers are built
3. Christopher Columbus
4. A map of Mexico
5. The meaning of the word *orchard*
6. What makes an airplane fly
7. A map of the world
8. Early inventions
9. The meaning of the word *wizard*
10. How gold was discovered
11. A map of the United States
12. The history of baseball
13. The first trip to the moon

Sample Answer 1. dictionary

Doing a Survey

Very often you need to gather and organize information. A *survey* is a way of gathering and organizing information.

Matt wants to find out which sport the children in his class like best. He did this survey. He asked the children to choose either baseball, swimming, or skating. He wrote down each child's answer. Then he counted all the answers to see what sport most children picked. Last he made a chart to show the children's answers.

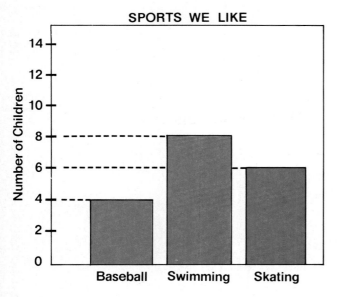

SPORTS WE LIKE

- Look at the chart.

  It shows that four children like baseball. Eight children like swimming. Six children like skating. The children in the class like swimming the best.

- Notice how Matt did his survey.

  He asked questions.
  He wrote down the answers.
  He counted all the different answers.
  He made a chart to show the answers.

Talk About It _____

Rosa did a survey. The chart shows the information
she gathered. Look at the chart. Which of these
questions did Rosa ask?

1. Who has a dog for a pet?
2. Who has a cat for a pet?
3. Who has a bird for a pet?
4. Who has no pets?

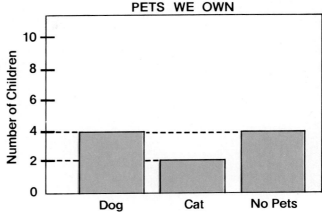

Skills Practice _____

Stan did a survey. The chart shows the information
he gathered. Look at the chart. Write a sentence to
answer each of these questions.

1. How many children
   like bananas?

2. How many children
   like apples?

3. How many children
   like oranges?

4. Which fruit do the
   children like best?

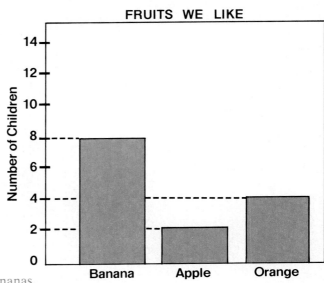

Sample Answer 1. Eight children like bananas.

Interviews and Reports

Thinking About Interviews and Reports

You have just won first place in a contest. You drew the best safety poster in your grade. There is going to be a story about you in the newspaper. A person from the newspaper comes to school to ask you some questions. The person is called a *reporter*.

- Look at the questions the reporter asks you.

> What is your name? How old are you? Who is your teacher? How did you get the idea for your poster? How long did it take you to make the poster?

The reporter used question words like *who, what, when, where, why,* and *how*. They help the reporter find out about you and the contest.

The reporter writes down all your answers. The questions and answers are called an *interview*. The reporter asks questions only about you and your poster. The reporter reads all the questions and answers in the interview very carefully. Then the reporter writes a report. The report tells about what you said.

Talking About Interviews and Reports

Paula wanted to write a report about playing soccer.
She interviewed a player on the school soccer team.
These are the questions Paula asked.

How many players are on the soccer team?
When does a team score points during a
game? What are some of the rules in soccer?

Paula got these answers:

There are eleven players on a soccer team. A
team scores points when the ball is kicked
past the goal line of the other team. Players
cannot touch the ball with their hands or arms
as they move down the field.

1. What is the first word in each question?
2. Why did Paula ask questions only about soccer?
3. What other questions could Paula ask?

Writing a Report

Pretend you want to write a report about being a
school nurse. Write four questions you could ask
your school nurse. Try to use question words like
who, what, why, where, when, and *how.*

A Class Report

Thinking About Reports

Your class is going to write a report together. Your report will be about Paula's soccer interview in the last lesson. You remember that Paula asked three questions about soccer. Here are the answers she got.

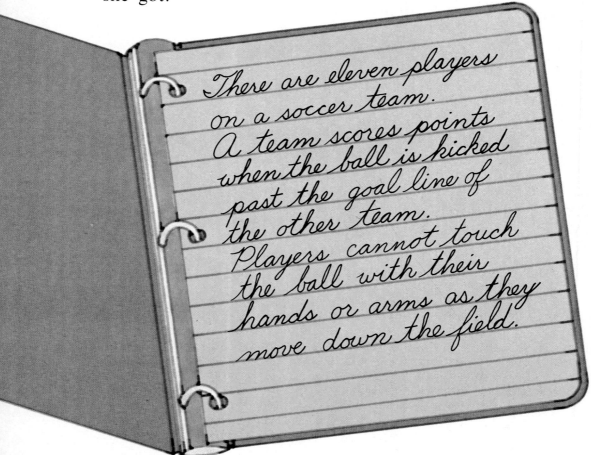

There are eleven players on a soccer team. A team scores points when the ball is kicked past the goal line of the other team. Players cannot touch the ball with their hands or arms as they move down the field.

Your report will use these answers. Your report should be one paragraph. You will need a main idea sentence. You can use the sentences above as your detail sentences.

Writing a Report

1. Your report will begin with a main idea sentence. Choose one of these sentences for the main idea sentence. Your teacher will write your report on the board.

Soccer is an interesting game to play.

There are many things to know about soccer.

2. Use Paula's first answer as the second sentence in your report.

3. Use Paula's second answer as the next sentence in your report.

4. Use Paula's third answer as the last sentence in your report.

5. Read your report. Does it tell some interesting things about soccer?

6. Write the finished report on your paper.

Careers

Do you like to read sports stories in newspapers and magazines? They are written by sports reporters. These people must know a lot about sports. They interview sports stars and watch games. They must write interesting reports about them. Good sports reporters can write very well. They have good ideas and know how to write them. If you want to be a reporter, you must be a good writer.

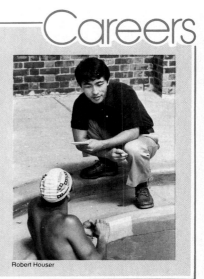

Robert Houser

Your Own Report

Thinking About Your Report

Now you will write a report of your own. Pretend you interviewed a basketball player. You asked the person many questions. They were about the game last night.

You wrote the answers to your questions. But the answers are not in the best order for putting them into your report. These are the answers in the order you wrote them:

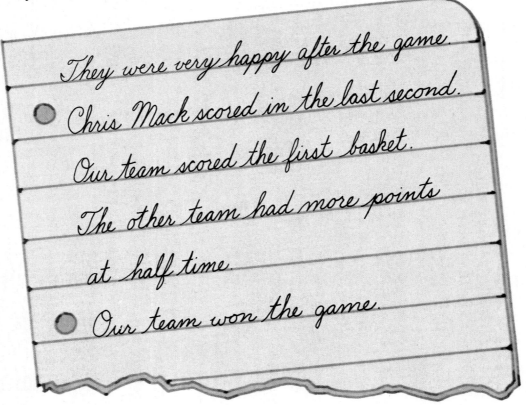

They were very happy after the game.
Chris Mack scored in the last second.
Our team scored the first basket.
The other team had more points at half time.
Our team won the game.

Your report will be a paragraph. You will need to change the order of the sentences to write your report.

Writing Your Report

1. Your report will start with a main idea sentence. Choose one of these sentences to be your main idea sentence. Write it on your paper.
   The basketball game last night was exciting.
   Everyone enjoyed the basketball game last night.

2. Look at the answers to the questions again. What is the best order of the sentences for your report? Write the sentences in that order. Your first sentence could be about which team scored first.

3. Read your report. Make sure it tells everything about the basketball game.

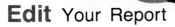

Edit Your Report

Read your report again. Think about these questions.

1. Does your report tell about one main idea?

2. Did you use any helping verbs in your sentences? Which ones did you use?

3. Did you use capital letters and periods where they were needed? Did you indent the first sentence?

Correct your mistakes. Make a good copy of your report.

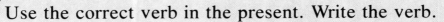

Checking Skills

Use the correct verb in the present. Write the verb.

pages 220-221

1. Lisa ___ the pots and pans. (wash)
2. Paul ___ them. (dry)
3. He ___ everything away. (put)
4. They ___ a broken dish. (fix)

Use the correct verb in the past. Write the verb. *pages 220-221*

5. The boy ___ very hard. (study)
6. He ___ for an easy test. (hope)
7. The girl ___ to play ball. (want)
8. She ___ some friends to play. (ask)

Write each verb. Then tell whether the verb is in the present, the past, or the future. *pages 222-223*

9. John bowls.
10. He will bowl on Saturday.
11. Akiko bowled last week.
12. Both teams will play soon.

Write the verb that names an action in the past. *pages 224-225*

13. Dora ___ breakfast early. (eat)
14. I ___ to school on the bus. (go)
15. You ___ our teacher. (see)
16. We ___ our homework last night. (do)

Write the helping verb and the verb. *pages 226-227*

17. My friend has joined the swim team.
18. She has learned to dive very well.
19. The swimmers have entered two races.

Complete each sentence. Write the correct form of the verb. *pages 226-227*

20. John has ___ many times.   (play)
21. Gail has ___ the game.   (start)
22. A child has ___ the winner.   (pick)

Complete each sentence. Write the correct form of the verb. *pages 228-229*

23. The boy has ___ us home.   (take)
24. He has ___ to the movies.   (go)
25. The girl has ___ the same movie.   (see)
26. They have ___ their jobs.   (begin)

Read each sentence using a contraction for the underlined words. Write the contraction.   *pages 232-233*

27. You <u>do not</u> know Carlos.   **28.** I <u>can not</u> play now.

You want to write a report about germs. You plan to interview the school nurse. Read these questions. Write the four questions that you should ask in the interview. *pages 246-249*

29. **a.** Where do germs come from?
    b. How do germs get in our bodies?
    c. What color is your office painted?
    d. When can germs do the most harm?
    e. Who are some famous people you have met?
    f. Why can't we see germs?

A True Story

Many stories often tell about real people. This story was written by a girl from Hong Kong. Now she lives in the United States. She can write English very well. But she wants to keep speaking and writing Chinese, too. She knows that it is important to know another language. So she goes to two schools every day. Read about what she is learning in her Chinese school.

Ingbert Grüttner

CHINESE BRUSH PAINTING

My name is Wynne Lee, and I started to learn Chinese brush painting when I was six years old. It takes a long time to learn.

I learned Chinese and English in Hong Kong. I've been in the United States for four years. Here I go to an American school, and then every afternoon from 4:30 to 7 I go to a Chinese school.

I brought an ink box with me from Hong Kong, but you can buy them in the United States. The box has cotton in it. You pour special writing ink into the box and you use a special brush.

Chinese is written from top to bottom and from left to right. Some Chinese words sound almost alike. Some look alike, too.

You hold the brush straight up. The real Chinese way is to write with the pen just under your nose, but most children don't do that. It's very hard.

Wynne Lee

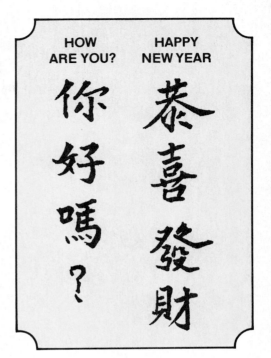

HOW ARE YOU?

HAPPY NEW YEAR

你好嗎?

恭喜發財

Activities

1. **Creative Writing** Wynne Lee knows how to write in two different ways. She can write the way you do. She can write in Chinese, too. You can write in two different ways, too. One way is with letters. Another is with your own pictures. Write a sentence that tells what you like to do when you have a vacation. On another piece of paper, draw a picture of what you like to do when you have a vacation.

2. Wynne Lee traveled a long way to get to the United States. She went from Hong Kong to Japan. Then she went to Hawaii. Finally she arrived in California. Use a class map. Use your finger to trace Wynne Lee's trip from Hong Kong to California.

Grammar and Related Language Skills

Review of Sentences
Nouns and Pronouns in Sentences
Verbs in Sentences
Sentence Building

Practical Communication

Learning About Facts and Opinions
Writing a Book Report

Creative Expression

A Story

255

Three Kinds of Sentences

You have learned many things about sentences. A *sentence* is a group of words that states a complete idea. Some sentences tell something. Some sentences ask something. Some sentences show strong feeling.

A **telling sentence** is a sentence that tells something.

A **question sentence** is a sentence that asks something.

An **exclamation sentence** is a sentence that shows strong feeling.

Christina's World by Andrew Wyeth (1948)

● Read each sentence about the picture. Is it a telling sentence, a question sentence, or an exclamation sentence?

How beautiful the painting is!
A girl sits in the grass.
Do you see a house?
Who painted the picture?

When you write a sentence, you must begin and end it with special signs.

Use a **capital letter** to begin the first word of each sentence.

Use a **period** (.) at the end of a telling sentence.

Use a **question mark** (**?**) at the end of a question sentence.

Use an **exclamation mark** (**!**) at the end of an exclamation sentence.

Talk About It

Read each sentence. Is it a telling sentence, a question sentence, or an exclamation sentence? What special signs are missing?

1. I play the drums
2. the drum is broken
3. who broke it
4. What a good song that is

Skills Practice

Write each sentence correctly. Write **telling** if it is a telling sentence. Write **question** if it is a question sentence. Write **exclamation** if it is an exclamation sentence.

1. Have you read this story
2. a young girl grows up in the city.
3. her grandfather lives in the mountains
4. does she visit him
5. what a long trip it is
6. how happy she is

Writing Sentences

Think of a story you read. Write one telling sentence about the story. Write one question sentence about it. Write one exclamation sentence about it.

Sample Answer 1. Have you read this story? question

Nouns and Pronouns in the Subject Part

Every sentence has two parts. They work together to state a complete idea. The *subject part* of a sentence names whom or what the sentence is about. The *predicate part* of a sentence tells what action the subject part does.

- Look at this sentence. The blue part is the subject part. The red part is the predicate part.

  Our class | put on a show.

Now you will take a closer look at the subject part of a sentence. Every subject has a noun or a pronoun. Words like *doctor, school,* and *car* are nouns. Words like *he, I,* and *they* are pronouns.

> A **noun** is a word that names a person, a place, or a thing.

> A **pronoun** is a word that takes the place of one or more nouns.

The subject part may have more than one word. The noun or pronoun is always the main word.

- Read each sentence. Look at the subject part. What is the main word in the subject part? Is it a noun or a pronoun?

  The boy | played music.   Sandy | clapped.

  He | blew a horn.   She | liked the song.

Talk About It

Read each sentence. What is the main word in the subject part? Is it a noun or a pronoun?

1. Ron tripped.
2. He fell.
3. Two dancers helped.
4. They pulled Ron up.

Skills Practice

Write each sentence. Draw a line between the subject part and the predicate part.

1. Pam goes to dancing school.
2. Jerry goes, too.
3. He jumps high in the air.
4. She moves across the floor quickly.
5. The children wear special clothes.
6. They practice everyday.

Read each sentence. Write the main word in the subject part. Then write **noun** if the word is a noun. Write **pronoun** if the word is a pronoun.

7. My mother took me to a show.
8. We saw many people.
9. A man told funny jokes.
10. He made us laugh.
11. A woman sang two songs.
12. Some people acted in a short play.
13. It made us laugh, too.
14. I had a good time.

Sample Answers 1. Pam | goes to dancing school. **7.** mother, noun

Verbs in Sentences

You have looked at the words in the subject part of a sentence. The main word in the subject part is a noun or a pronoun.

Now look at the predicate part. Remember, the *predicate part* of a sentence tells what action the subject part does. Every predicate part has a verb.

A **verb** is a word that names an action.

The predicate part may have more than one word. But the main word in the predicate part is the verb.

- Read each sentence. Look at the predicate part. What is the verb?

Susan | sang.

I | played the drums.

We | acted in a play, too.

Talk About It

Read each sentence. Find the verb.

1. Our class made costumes.
2. Anita cut the cloth.
3. Joe sewed with a needle.
4. Then we ironed them.
5. Maria sang a song.
6. Ted danced.
7. Jim clapped his hands.
8. They all laughed.

Skills Practice

Write each sentence. Underline the verb.

1. Roy draws a picture.
2. He paints carefully.
3. He colors a house red.
4. The picture hangs on the wall.
5. Peter writes stories.
6. He reads a story to the class.
7. They talk about the story.
8. Some children ask questions.
9. The class adds other sentences.
10. The teacher tells the class his ideas.

Writing Sentences

Pretend you saw a magic show. Write two sentences about the show. Use a noun in the subject part of one sentence. Use a pronoun in the subject part of the other sentence. Be sure to use a verb in each predicate part.

Sample Answer 1. Roy <u>draws</u> a picture.

Building Sentences

Every sentence you write must have a noun or a pronoun in the subject part. These words name whom or what the sentence is about.

NOUN   **PRONOUN**

The boxed children | dance.   boxed We | watch.

You can add other words to make your sentences tell more. Sometimes you want to tell more about a noun. Then you may add words to the subject part. You already know that you may add adjectives.

An **adjective** is a word that describes a noun.

● Read these sentences.

boxed The four children | dance.
boxed The little children | dance.
boxed The happy children | dance.

The adjectives *four, little,* and *happy* were added to the subject part of the sentences. They describe the noun *children*. Each *adjective* tells you more about the children.

Every sentence must have a verb in the predicate part. The verb names the action the noun or pronoun does.

NOUN   **VERB**   **PRONOUN VERB**

A rabbit | boxed hops.   I | boxed laugh.

Sometimes you add words to the predicate part.
They help tell more about the action of the verb.

- Read these sentences.

The children | dance together.   We | watch the children.
The children | dance fast.   We | watch quietly.

Some words were added to the predicate part of the
sentences. They come after the verb in each
sentence. The words tell more about the action of
the verb. They tell *how* the children dance. They
tell *whom* we watch and *how* we watch.

Talk About It

Read each sentence. Add more words to the subject
part or the predicate part to make a good sentence.

1. The boys played.   **2.** Our parents read.

Skills Practice

Add words to the subject part of each sentence.
Then write the sentence.

1. The wind blew.   **3.** A parade passed.
2. A lion roared.   **4.** The children followed.

Add words to the predicate part of each sentence.
Then write the sentence.

5. Carol walked.   **7.** Stan drives.
6. I rode.   **8.** We fly.

Understanding New Words

Sometimes you may not know the meaning of a word in a sentence. You can look up the word in the dictionary. You can also look at the other words in the sentence. Sometimes the other words help you understand the meaning of a word.

● Read this sentence.

They gave me a nice *reward* for finding the puppy.

Suppose you did not know the meaning of *reward*. Read the sentence again. The other words in the sentence give you an idea of what *reward* means. A *reward* is something given to you in return for something good that you did.

Sometimes you have to read the sentences before and after the word to find its meaning. The other sentences can help make the meaning of the word clear.

● Read these sentences.

Nicky thinks the soup tastes good.
Dolores thinks so, too.
She *agrees* with Nicky.

Read the sentences again. They tell you that both Nicky and Dolores like the soup. The word *agrees* tells you Dolores feels the same way about the soup as Nicky does.

Talk About It

Read each sentence. Try to find out the meaning of the underlined word.

1. My <u>assistant</u> will help me do the magic show.
2. I want to have a party to <u>celebrate</u> my birthday.
3. The fish is very <u>slippery</u>.
   The fish slid right out of my hand.
4. Tim just moved in.
   He is a <u>newcomer</u> on our street.

Skills Practice

Read each sentence. Write the underlined word in each sentence. Write what you think the word means.

1. Bill washed the shirt to <u>remove</u> the spot on it.
2. The balloon <u>burst</u> when I put too much air in it.
3. The fire <u>occurred</u> early in the morning.
4. I want a glass of water to drink. I am <u>thirsty</u>.
5. Myra did not sleep well.
   The bed had a lumpy <u>mattress</u>.
6. I put the letter in an <u>envelope</u>.
   Then I wrote your name and address on it.
7. Nana is my <u>companion</u>.
   She goes everywhere with me.

Skills Review

Write each sentence correctly. Then write **telling** if it is a telling sentence. Write **question** if it is a question sentence. Write **exclamation** if it is an exclamation sentence.

1. my friends played records
2. What songs do they like
3. how beautiful the music is
4. Cathy hears the loud horns
5. Who listens to the piano
6. What a pretty song that is

Read each sentence. Write the main word in the subject part. Then write **noun** if the word is a noun. Write **pronoun** if the word is a pronoun.

7. Karen plays the piano.
8. She practices every day.
9. Her sister writes lovely songs.
10. They sing in a contest.
11. John bakes bread.
12. He mixes the flour completely.
13. His mother adds the water.
14. They cook in the kitchen.

Read each sentence. Write the verb.

15. My brother climbs mountains.
16. He jumps rope, too.
17. My sister skates everyday.

18. She runs every morning.

19. They enter many races.

Add more words to the subject part of each sentence. Then write the sentence.

20. The boys look.   **21.** A dog jumps.

Add more words to the predicate part of each sentence. Then write the sentence.

22. Ms. Bridge drives.   **23.** My uncles cut.

Read each sentence. Write the underlined word in each sentence. Write what you think the word means.

24. The kitten <u>trembled</u> as the noise grew louder.

25. We need to <u>breathe</u> air to live.

26. There were not many children at school.
Only a <u>handful</u> came.

27. They went to the school play. We also <u>attended</u>.

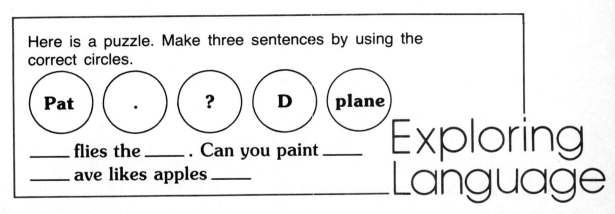

Here is a puzzle. Make three sentences by using the correct circles.

(**Pat**) (**.**) (**?**) (**D**) (**plane**)

_____ flies the _____ . Can you paint _____

_____ ave likes apples _____

Exploring Language

Fact and Opinion

You often read and hear what people have to say. Sometimes they state facts. A *fact* gives information that is true. Facts can also be checked. Sometimes people give opinions. An *opinion* tells what people think or feel.

The woman on TV is stating facts. You can check if the information about the rocket is true. All the children are giving opinions. They tell what they think or feel about the rocket trip.

Wayne and his sister went to the museum. Here are some things they said.

Birds lay eggs in their nests.
Some birds make nests from grass.
These are interesting birds.
Their feathers are beautiful.

● Read the sentences again. Which sentences state facts? Which give opinions?

Talk About It

Read each sentence. Does it state a fact or an opinion?

1. Many fish live in the sea.
2. Bluefish are the prettiest fish.
3. Scientists explore the sea.
4. Exploring the sea must be exciting.

Skills Practice

Write **fact** if the sentence states a fact. Write **opinion** if the sentence gives an opinion.

1. There are four seasons in the year.
2. Spring is the best season.
3. Flowers come out in the spring.
4. Leaves fall in the autumn.
5. Fall leaves are beautiful.
6. It is hot in the summer.
7. Maybe it will be cooler this summer.
8. Flowers need rain to grow.
9. The trees get wet when it rains.
10. Rain is awful.

Sample Answer 1. Fact

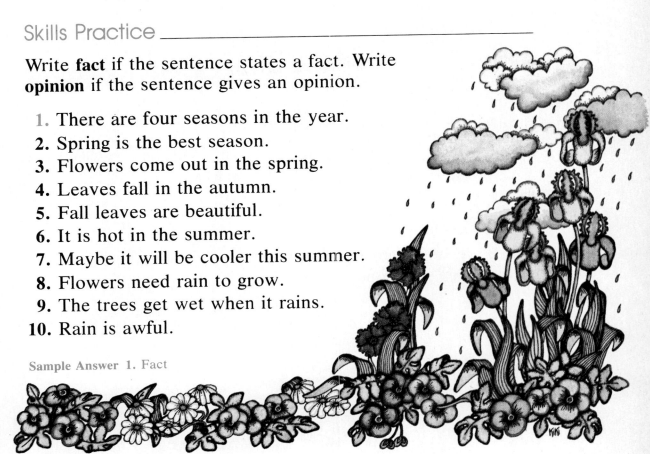

Ads

You have probably seen many ads before. *Ads* tell you about things you can buy. You can find ads on TV and radio. Newspapers and magazines also have ads. Some books have ads on their covers.

You'll love Circus Wheels. We've added nuts and fruits. Circus Wheels have important vitamins your body needs. They are good for you!

Many ads give facts. Facts give information that can be checked. Facts also give information that is helpful. Ads also state opinions. Opinions tell what someone thinks or feels.

- Look at the ad above. What does the ad tell you about? Which sentences state facts? Which sentences state opinions?

Here are sentences from another ad. This ad is on the cover of a book.

This book is about caring for your dog. It is the best book to read. The book tells how to train your dog. You'll enjoy reading this book.

● Look at the ad on the book cover again. What does the ad tell you about? Which sentences state facts? Which sentences state opinions?

Talk About It

Read this ad. Does each sentence state a fact or an opinion?

1. *Granny's Pies* are delicious!
2. They have vitamins.
3. They're better than any pies you've ever tasted.

Read this ad from a book jacket. Does each sentence state a fact or an opinion?

1. *Make Way for Ducklings* is a great book.
2. The family of ducks lives in Boston.
3. You'll love this story!
4. This story won an award.

Skills Practice

Read each ad. Write **fact** if the ad states a fact. Write **opinion** if it gives an opinion.

1. *Country Bread* is baked fresh everyday!
2. We make our bread with milk and flour.
3. We add butter, too.
4. Our bread is the best you can buy.
5. *Madeline* is the story of a little girl.
6. She lives in Paris.
7. This story is good.
8. The pictures are interesting.

Book Reports

Thinking About Book Reports

Sometimes the ad on the jacket of a book makes you want to read the book. When you like a book you want your friends to read it, too.

A *book report* tells other people about a book you have read. The report is done a certain way. First you tell the name of the book. This is the book's *title*. Next you tell who wrote the book. This person is the *author*. Then you tell what the book is about.

There are many ways to tell about a book. You can describe the people that are in the book. You can tell the order of things that happen in the book.

● Look at this book report.

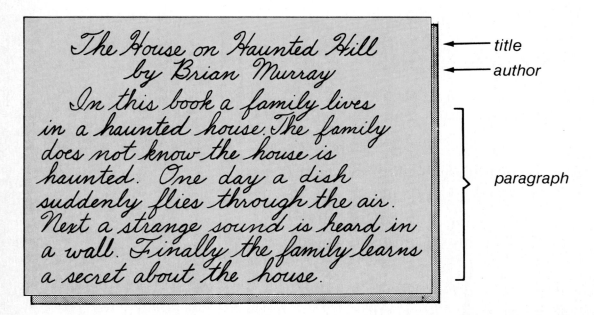

The House on Haunted Hill
by Brian Murray
In this book a family lives in a haunted house. The family does not know the house is haunted. One day a dish suddenly flies through the air. Next a strange sound is heard in a wall. Finally the family learns a secret about the house.

title — author — paragraph

Notice that the title of the book was written at the top of the page. The author's name was written next. Then the paragraph told about the book.

The first sentence in the paragraph gave the main idea of the whole book. The other sentences told the order of things that happened in the book.

Notice that the book report did not tell the entire story. If it did, the report would be too long. Also, people might not read the book if they already knew everything that happened.

Talking About Book Reports

Read the book report on the other page.

1. What is the title of the book?
2. Who is the author?
3. What is the book about?
4. Did the paragraph describe a person or tell about things in time order?

Writing a Book Report

The information below belongs in a book report. But it is not in the right order. Write the information in the right order.

This book is about how to care for a dog.
I learned three things.
Last you must give your dog a nice place to sleep.
First you must feed a dog good food every day.
Next you must give your dog some exercise.
Lila Berger
Your New Dog

Your Own Book Report

Thinking About Your Book Report

Now you will write your own book report. Choose a book you have read and liked. Think about what you want to tell about your book. Try not to tell the whole story. Do not tell how the book ends.

Writing Your Book Report

Use this form to help you write your book report.

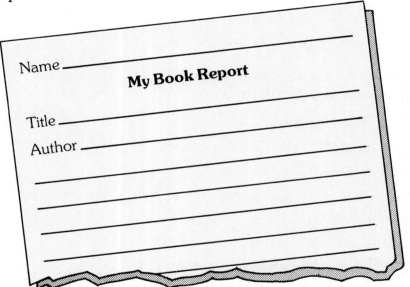

1. Write your name on the top of your paper.
2. Write the title of the book. Write the name of the author.
3. Write a main idea sentence about the book. Remember to indent the first word.
4. Write three or four detail sentences. Tell what happened in the book.

Edit Your Book Report

Read the book report you have written. Think about these questions as you read.

1. Did your book report tell something interesting about the book?

2. Did you use a good main idea sentence?

3. Did you spell the title of the book correctly? Did you spell the author's name correctly?

4. Did you use capital letters and periods correctly?

A Book Talk

Sometimes you want to share your book report with your class. You can read your book report or you can tell about the book in your own words.

Your class will enjoy your book report more if you follow these rules.

1. Look at the people in the class as you speak.

2. Speak loudly enough for everyone to hear you.

3. Do not speak too fast. Speak clearly so people will understand you.

4. Tell people where they can find the book. They may want to read it.

Remember to be a good listener when someone shares a book report. Try to follow these rules.

1. Look at the person. Do not talk to other people.

2. Try to remember what the person is saying.

3. Ask questions at the end about things you did not understand.

Checking Skills

Write each sentence correctly. Then write **telling** if it is a telling sentence. Write **question** if it is a question sentence. Write **exclamation** if it is an exclamation sentence. *pages 256–257*

1. did you read this story?
2. how hard I cried
3. i drew a picture about the story
4. Do you like it
5. The teacher hung my picture on the wall
6. What a good story it was

Read each sentence. Write the main word in the subject part. Then write **noun** if the word is a noun. Write **pronoun** if the word is a pronoun. *pages 258–259*

7. A girl went to see her grandmother.
8. She wore a red cape.
9. A wolf saw her in the forest.
10. He wanted her basket.
11. It was filled with food.

Read each sentence. Write the verb. *pages 260–261*

12. I play the piano.
13. My sister sings.
14. We enjoy music.
15. We practice every day.
16. Our parents listen to us.

Add words to the subject part and the predicate part of each sentence. Then write the sentence. *pages 262–263*

17. The band played.   **20.** People stood.
18. The children sang.   **21.** A man cheered.
19. A girl danced.   **22.** A woman clapped.

Write the underlined word in each sentence. Write what you think the word means. *pages 264–265*

23. I forgot your book.
Please <u>remind</u> me to get it.

24. There is no one home.
I feel very <u>lonely</u>.

The information below belongs in a book report. But it is not in the right order. Find the book's title and author. Put the sentences in the right order. *pages 272–275*

25. a. The Monroe family took an interesting trip.
b. The family started their trip in the fall.
c. by Margaret Hope
d. They got stuck in snow in the winter.
e. Finally the Monroes returned home in the summer.
f. A Year to Remember
g. They traveled around the world in one year.
h. Next the family got lost in the spring.

26. Write the book report.

Has anyone ever whispered in your ear? Sometimes you do not hear the whole message. In this story, whispering leads to one mix-up after another. All the animals know only one thing for sure. "It's a surprise!"

The Surprise Party

"I'm having a party tomorrow," whispered Rabbit.
"It's a surprise."

"Rabbit is hoeing the parsley tomorrow," whispered Owl.
"It's a surprise."

"Rabbit is going to sea tomorrow," whispered Squirrel.
"It's a surprise."

"Rabbit is climbing a tree tomorrow," whispered Duck.
"It's a surprise."

"Rabbit is riding a flea tomorrow," whispered Mouse. "It's a surprise."

"Rabbit is raiding the poultry tomorrow," whispered Fox. "It's a surprise."

"Reading poetry?" said Frog to himself.
"His own, I suppose. How dull."

The next day Rabbit went to see Frog.
"Come with me, Frog," he said.
"I have a surprise for you."
"No, thank you," said Frog.
"I know your poetry. It puts me to sleep."
And he hopped away.

So Rabbit went to see Fox.
"Come with me, Fox," he said.
"I have a surprise for you."
"No, thank you," said Fox.
"I don't want you raiding the poultry.
I'll get the blame."
And he ran off.

So Rabbit went to see Mouse.
"Come with me Mouse," he said.
"I have a surprise for you."
"No, thank you," said Mouse.

"A rabbit riding a flea?
Even I am too big for that."
And Mouse scampered away.

So Rabbit went to see Duck.
"Come with me, Duck," he said.
"I have a surprise for you."
"No, thank you," said Duck.
"Mouse told me you were climbing a tree.
Really, you're too old for that sort of thing."
And Duck waddled off.

So Rabbit went to see Squirrel.
"Come with me, Squirrel,"
he said.
"I have a surprise for you."
"No, thank you," said Squirrel.
"I know you're going to sea, but good-byes make me sad."
And Squirrel ran up the tree.

So Rabbit went to see Owl.

"Owl," he said, "I don't know what YOU think
I'm doing, but "I'M HAVING A PARTY."
And this time everyone heard clearly.
"A party!" they shouted. "Why didn't you say so?"
"A party! How nice!" And it was a nice party.
And such a surprise.

Pat Hutchins

I'm Having A PARTY!

Activities —————————————————————

1. This story would make a good puppet play.
   Choose classmates to play the part of each
   animal. Each classmate will draw the animal he
   or she will play. Color the animals and cut them
   out. Your class will need some sticks or long,
   narrow pieces of wood. Fasten the animals to the
   stick. Act out the play using the puppets. Each
   classmate should read what the animal says in the
   story.

2. **Creative Writing** Read the story again. Tell what
   words each animal changes in each message. Then
   write some other mixed-up messages. Here is one.

   "I am making a flower," whispered Bob.
   "Bob is taking a shower," whispered Dave.

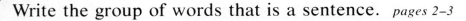

End-of-Year Review

Write the group of words that is a sentence. *pages 2–3*

1. A lion roared.
   A lion.
2. A deer.
   A deer ran.

3. An elephant.
   An elephant ate hay.
4. The animals ate.
   The animals.

Write each sentence correctly. Then write **telling**
if it is a telling sentence. Write **question** if it is
a question sentence. Write **exclamation** if it is an
exclamation sentence. *pages 6–7, 8–9*

5. joe called Pete today.
6. can you go to Lee Park

7. what fun we can have
8. al will be here at noon

Look at the part in the box. Write **subject** or
predicate if it is a subject part or predicate part. *pages 12–13*

9. The animals | slept.

10. The keeper | fed them.

Write the nouns. Write **singular** if the noun is
singular. Write **plural** if it is plural. *pages 36-37*

11. The lion has a cub.
12. The boys played ball.

13. The elephants ate nuts.
14. The girl flew a kite.

Write each noun. Write **proper** if it is a proper noun.
Write **common** if it is a common noun. *pages 48-49*

15. Ira went to Central Store.
16. Juan sang songs.

17. A dog followed Ira.
18. Inez walked to Hill Drive.

Write each name and address correctly. *pages 50-53*

19. mr ron c madsen
89 oak street
cleveland ohio 44121

20. mrs h ortez
319 sterling road
houston texas 77007

Write each date correctly. *pages 52-53*

21. may 16 1983
22. july 10 1981

23. april 24 1980
24. march 8 1982

Write the correct verb in the present. *pages 78-79*

25. Rob ___ hard. (try)
26. Sue ___ the pot. (wash)

Write the correct verb in the past. *pages 84-85*

27. Xi ___ them. (call)
28. Jaime ___ fish. (fry)

Complete each sentence that has a blank. Write
the pronoun. *pages 116-117, 120-121*

29. The boys clean the floor.
___ use a can of wax.

30. Pearl dusts the room.
___ uses a cloth.

31. The boys paint pictures.
___ sister helps them. (His, Their)

32. ___ brush moves quickly. (Her, Its)

Write the correct verb in each sentence. *pages 118-119*

33. They ___ the stairs. (sweep, sweeps)
34. He ___ the bed. (make, makes)
35. You ___ the dishes. (dry, dries)

Look at the noun in ( ). Use the possessive form of the noun in the blank. Write the possessive noun. *pages 154-155, 158-159*

36. The ___ bikes had bells.   (boys)
37. One ___ bike had a flag.   (girl)
38. The ___ bike had a horn.   (woman)

Write each sentence correctly. Use a capital letter to begin each important word in a proper noun. *pages 162-163*

39. I swim in june and july.
40. We had fun on friday.
41. This sunday is mother's day.
42. I saw you in april.

Write each adjective and the noun it describes. *pages 184-185*

43. I saw a red balloon.
44. A little boy held it.
45. The dog had sad eyes.
46. A big girl threw a ball.

Write an adjective to complete each sentence. *pages 186-187*

47. We went to a ___ park.
48. She wore a ___ hat.
49. I carried a ___ ball.
50. Ted saw a ___ cat.

Write the correct adjective to fill each blank. *pages 188-189*

51. Bev found an old coin.
   Bob found an ___ coin than Bev's.   (older, oldest)
52. Miguel got the ___ coin of all.   (older, oldest)
53. Sue had a soft pillow.
   Lois had a ___ pillow.   (softest, softer)

Use a correct article. Write the article. *page 191*

54. Matt had ___ wagon.   **56.** ___ wheels are rubber.
55. ___ wagon has wheels.   **57.** It is___ orange wagon.

Write each verb. Then write whether the verb is in
the **present,** the **past,** or the **future.** *pages 222-223*

58. Rita played golf.   **60.** Rita tries very hard.
59. She will play again soon.   **61.** She learns quickly.

Write the verb that names an action in the past. *pages 224-225*

62. I ___ the bus. (see)   **64.** Two girls ___ home. (go)
63. Lisa ___ lunch. (eat)   **65.** I ___, too. (do)

Write the correct form of the verb. *pages 226-227*

66. Liz has ___ home. (go)   **68.** I have ___ Joe. (see)
67. She has ___ dinner. (eat)   **69.** Val has ___ well. (do)

Write the main word in the subject part. Write **noun**
if it is a noun. Write **pronoun** if it is a pronoun. *pages 258–259*

70. The girls play ball.   **72.** Mother bought a comb.
71. They had a bat.   **73.** It lasted a year.

Add words to the subject part and predicate part of
each sentence. Then write the sentence. *pages 262–263*

74. A woman ran.   **76.** A boy called.
75. The child laughed.   **77.** The dog played.

Table of Contents

I. GRAMMAR AND USAGE

Sentences

DEFINITION

A **sentence** is a group of words that state a complete idea. page 2 MORE PRACTICE, page 294

The farmer grows food for people.
Many animals live on a farm.

KINDS OF SENTENCES

A **telling sentence** is a sentence that tells something. page 6 MORE PRACTICE, pages 294, 300, 308
A robin built a nest.   The bird sings to me.

A **question sentence** is a sentence that asks something. page 6 MORE PRACTICE, pages 294, 300, 308
Why do birds sing?   Did you plant the tree?

An **exclamation sentence** is a sentence that shows strong feeling. page 6 MORE PRACTICE, pages 294, 300, 308
How pretty the song is!   What a tall tree that is!

PART OF SENTENCES

The **subject part** of a sentence names whom or what the sentence is about. page 12 MORE PRACTICE, pages 295, 300, 309
<u>Rosa</u> jumped rope.   <u>The children</u> played tag.

The **predicate part** of a sentence tells what action the subject part does. page 12 MORE PRACTICE, pages 295, 300, 309
The cat <u>pawed the sofa</u>.   Jack <u>chased the cat</u>.

Parts of Speech

NOUN

A **noun** is a word that names a person, a place, or a thing. page 36 MORE PRACTICE, pages 295, 308

The <u>neighbor</u> came to our <u>house</u>.
The <u>door</u> blew shut in my <u>face</u>.

A **singular noun** is a noun that names one person, place, or thing. page 40 MORE PRACTICE, pages 296, 302

A <u>child</u> threw a <u>ball</u>.
An old <u>woman</u> walked by the <u>house</u>.

A **plural noun** is a noun that names more than one person, place, or thing. Most plural nouns have **s** or **es** endings. page 40 MORE PRACTICE, pages 296, 302

The wild <u>animals</u> sat in the <u>cages</u>.
Tami put the <u>kittens</u> in two <u>boxes</u>.

Use **the** before singular or plural nouns. page 191 MORE PRACTICE, page 305

Joanna set <u>the</u> table.

Mother washed <u>the</u> dishes.

Use **a** and **an** before singular nouns only. Use **an** before words that begin with vowel sounds. Use **a** before words that begin with all other sounds. page 191 MORE PRACTICE, page 305

Alice saw <u>a</u> squirrel in <u>a</u> tree.

She saw it eating <u>an</u> acorn.

A **common noun** is a noun that names any person, place, or thing. page 48 MORE PRACTICE, pages 297, 302

The <u>boy</u> plays with a <u>dog</u>.

The <u>dog</u> sleeps under the <u>bench</u>.

A **proper noun** is a noun that names a special person, place, or thing. Each important word in a proper noun begins with a capital letter. page 48 MORE PRACTICE, pages 297, 302

Many people visited the <u>Old West Museum</u>.

<u>Karen Cook</u> works in a store.

A **possessive noun** is a noun that names whom or what has something. page 150 MORE PRACTICE, page 303

Grandfather fixed <u>Tom's</u> bike.

He moved the <u>children's</u> toys.

PRONOUN

A **pronoun** is a word that takes the place of one or more nouns. page 116 MORE PRACTICE, pages 301, 308

Molly threw the ball. <u>She</u> threw the ball.

Tom caught the ball. <u>He</u> caught the ball.

Use **I** when you talk about yourself. page 118 MORE PRACTICE, page 301

May <u>I</u> change places with Agnes?

<u>I</u> want to see the pictures.

Use **we** when you talk about yourself and someone else. page 118 MORE PRACTICE, page 301

Can <u>we</u> play the game?   <u>We</u> can ask Mary to play.

Use **you** when you talk to another person. page 118 MORE PRACTICE, page 301
You must pay for the food.
Can you drive more slowly?

Use **you** when you talk to more than one person. page 118 MORE PRACTICE, page 301
You may stay with your mothers.
Can you beat that team tonight?

VERB

A **verb** is a word that names an action. page 70 MORE PRACTICE, page 298
The children jump.   Michael moves his chair.

A **verb in the present** names an action that happens now. page 74 MORE PRACTICE, pages 298, 306
Now the boy throws a ball.   The dog swims after the ball.

Add **s** to most verbs in the present when they work with singular nouns. page 78 MORE PRACTICE, page 299
Mother rides a bus to work.   Father walks to his office.

Do not change verbs in the present to make them work with plural nouns. page 81 MORE PRACTICE, page 299
The cowboys saddle the horses.   The animals kick the doors.

Add **ed** to most verbs to make a verb in the past. page 84 MORE PRACTICE, page 299
The band marched.
People called to the band.

A **verb in the past** names an action that happened before. page 82 MORE PRACTICE, pages 299, 306, 307
Yesterday, the bus stopped.
The children climbed the steps.

The **future tense of a verb** names an action that will take place in the future. page 222 MORE PRACTICE, page 306
Joan will swim in the race today.
Pedro will read three books this week.

A **helping verb** is a word that helps a verb to name an action. page 226 MORE PRACTICE, page 307
The family has moved to another city.
They have lived here for years.

Handbook

Add **ed** to most verbs when you use them with the helping verb **have** or **has**. page 228 MORE PRACTICE, page 307

You have learn<u>ed</u> the rules.

Robert has play<u>ed</u> the game many times.

ADJECTIVE

An **adjective** is a word that describes a noun. page 184 MORE PRACTICE, pages 304, 305

Little Tommy lives in a <u>big</u> house.

<u>Beautiful</u> flowers grow along the <u>green</u> fence.

Add **er** to an adjective to compare one thing with another. page 188 MORE PRACTICE, page 304

John saw a tall<u>er</u> tree than Sue did.

Add **est** to an adjective to compare several things. page 188 MORE PRACTICE, page 304

Jane found the tall<u>est</u> tree of all.

II. MECHANICS

Capitalization

Use a **capital letter** to begin the first word of every sentence. page 8 MORE PRACTICE, page 295

<u>T</u>he bride carried white flowers.   <u>P</u>eople waved at the car.

Begin each important word in a proper noun with a capital letter. page 50 MORE PRACTICE, pages 297, 302

<u>M</u>r. <u>F</u>rank <u>H</u>ess builds houses for people.

<u>T</u>he <u>D</u>oyles stopped to eat at <u>J</u>oe's <u>D</u>iner.

Begin a **title** with a capital letter. End most titles with a period. page 50 MORE PRACTICE, page 297

<u>Dr.</u> William Barnes cares for sick persons.

<u>Ms.</u> Martha Herr teaches the third grade.

An **initial** is the first letter of a name. Write an initial with a capital letter. Put a period after the letter. page 50 MORE PRACTICE, page 297

Maria <u>L.</u> Garcia is my friend.

<u>T. H.</u> White writes books.

Use **capital letters** to begin proper nouns that name places. page 52   MORE PRACTICE, page 297

The family visited <u>S</u>an <u>D</u>iego, <u>C</u>alifornia.
The <u>M</u>ississippi <u>R</u>iver flows south.

Punctuation

Use a **period** (.) at the end of a telling sentence. page 8   MORE PRACTICE, page 295

A heavy rain fell in the morning<u>.</u>
The Anderson family played games<u>.</u>

Use a **question mark** (?) at the end of a question sentence. page 9   MORE PRACTICE, page 295

Will you buy a bird<u>?</u>   Who bought the bird<u>?</u>

Use an **exclamation mark** (!) at the end of an exclamation sentence. page 9   MORE PRACTICE, page 295

How small the bird is<u>!</u>   What a big building<u>!</u>

Put a **comma** (,) between the name of the city and the state when you write them together. page 52   MORE PRACTICE, 297

I live in Waco<u>,</u> Texas.
You live in At<u>h</u>ens<u>,</u> Ohio.

Use a **comma** (,) to separate the day of the month from the year. page 53   MORE PRACTICE, page 297

January 3<u>,</u> 1982   April 10<u>,</u> 1981

Add an **apostrophe** and **s** ('s) to write the possessive of most singular nouns. page 152   MORE PRACTICE, page 303

What is the boy<u>'</u>s name? Jack took the giant<u>'</u>s gold.

Add an **apostrophe** (') to write the possessive of most plural nouns. page 153   MORE PRACTICE, page 303

Aunt Jenny sewed the girls<u>'</u> dresses.
Then she ironed the boys<u>'</u> pants.

Use an **apostrophe** (') in a contraction to take the place of the letter or letters that are left out. page 232   MORE PRACTICE, page 307

Don<u>'</u>t write in this book.
I can<u>'</u>t find my pencil.

III. SPELLING

Spelling Nouns

To make most singular nouns plural, add **s**. page 42 MORE PRACTICE, page 296

boy	girl	wagon
boys	girls	wagons

If a singular noun ends with **s, ss, x, ch,** or **sh, add es** to write the plural. page 42 MORE PRACTICE, page 296

lunch	bus	fox
lunches	buses	foxes

If a singular noun ends with a consonant and **y,** change the **y** to **i** and add **es** to write the plural. page 43 MORE PRACTICE, page 296

baby	penny	city
babies	pennies	cities

Spelling Verbs

If a verb ends in **s, ss, ch, sh,** or **x,** add **es** to make the verb work with a singular noun. page 78 MORE PRACTICE, page 299

toss	catch	fix
tosses	catches	fixes

If a verb ends with a consonant and **y,** change the **y** to **i** and add **es** to make the correct form of the present. page 79 MORE PRACTICE, page 299

cry	try	hurry
cries	tries	hurries

If the verb ends with a consonant and **y,** change the **y** to **i** and add **ed** to make a verb in the past. page 84 MORE PRACTICE, page 299

cry	hurry	try
cried	hurried	tried

If a verb ends with **e,** drop the **e** and add **ed** to make the correct form of the past. page 84 MORE PRACTICE, page 299

shape	use	vote
shaped	used	voted

Spelling Adjectives

If a word ends with consonant, vowel, consonant, double the last consonant and add **y** to form the adjective. page 196 MORE PRACTICE, page 305

fun	mud	sun
funny	muddy	sunny

IV. VOCABULARY

A **synonym** is a word that has nearly the same meaning as another word. page 194 MORE PRACTICE, page 305

Trees grow in the <u>forest</u>.
Trees grow in the <u>woods</u>.
The race <u>began</u> at noon.
The race <u>started</u> at noon.

An **antonym** is a word that means the opposite of another word. page 195 MORE PRACTICE, page 305

The <u>little</u> bears slept.
The <u>big</u> bears slept.
Bob wears his <u>old</u> shirt.
Bob wears his <u>new</u> shirt.

A **contraction** is a word made up of two words. The words are joined together to make one word. One or more letters are left out. page 232 MORE PRACTICE, page 307

<u>You're</u> very kind to me.
Lily <u>isn't</u> out of bed yet.

A **prefix** is a group of letters added to the beginning of a word. page 234

The <u>un</u>happy child cried.
You must <u>re</u>write the lesson.

Looking at Sentences, pages 2–5

Read the groups of words in each pair. Write each group of words that is a sentence.

1. Many animals live here.
   Many animals.

2. A squirrel.
   A squirrel eats a nut.

3. A rabbit eats the grass.
   A rabbit.

4. The birds build a nest.
   The birds.

5. Some ducks.
   Some ducks walk away.

6. A fish.
   A fish swims in the pond.

7. A frog jumps on a rock.
   A frog.

8. A cat sees a mouse.
   A cat.

9. Two dogs.
   Two dogs bark at a cat.

10. Some people walk quickly.
    Some people.

Three Kinds of Sentences, pages 6–7

Read each sentence. Write **telling** if it is a telling sentence. Write **question** if it is a question sentence. Write **exclamation** if it is an exclamation sentence.

1. We went to the pet store.
2. How small that puppy is!
3. Did you hear the bird?
4. What a pretty song it sings!
5. I liked the little monkey.
6. The monkey sat on my arm.
7. Did you see the kittens?
8. Did you buy a pet?

Beginning and Ending Sentences, pages 8–9

Some special signs are missing in each sentence.
Write each sentence correctly.

1. many bats live in caves
2. how dark this cave is!
3. When do bats hunt
4. they hunt at night.
5. What do bats eat

6. Bats hang upside down
7. bears live in caves.
8. Many sleep all winter
9. what a big bear that is
10. can you run fast

Subject Parts and Predicate Parts, pages 12–15

Read each sentence. Look at the part in the box.
Write **subject** if it is a subject part. Write **predicate**
if it is a predicate part.

1. The frog | found a ball.
2. A princess | lost it.
3. The frog | tossed the ball.
4. The princess | ran home.

5. The frog | knocked loudly.
6. The frog | came in.
7. The frog | sat quietly.
8. The frog | became a prince.

Looking at Nouns, pages 36–39

Read each sentence. Write each noun.

1. Jan went to the station.
2. Mother carried her bag.
3. Father bought a ticket.
4. Jan got on the bus.
5. A driver took the ticket.
6. Jan found a seat.

7. Jan sat near a window.
8. Her little brother waved.
9. The bus left the station.
10. A truck passed the bus.
11. Aunt Sue met Jan in town.
12. Uncle Bob waved to Jan.

More Practice

Singular and Plural Nouns, pages 40–41

Write each sentence with the correct noun.

1. Two ____ got on the bus. (boy, boys)
2. They rode to a little ____. (town, towns)
3. They stopped at three ____. (store, stores)
4. Jim bought a ____ for his bike. (bell, bells)
5. Fred bought a ____. (game, games)
6. They also bought two ____. (apple, apples)
7. A ____ passed them. (truck, trucks)

Forming Plural Nouns, pages 42–44

Write the plural of each noun.

1. train
2. bus
3. woman
4. watch
5. baby
6. box
7. class
8. dish
9. tooth
10. goose
11. car
12. airplane
13. child
14. family
15. foot

Making New Words, page 45

Change the underlined word in each pair of sentences to tell what kind of work the person does. Write the second sentence with the new word.

1. Lee <u>paints</u> houses.
   Lee is a ____.
2. Tom <u>sings</u> old songs.
   Tom is a ____.
3. Ginny <u>dances</u> in the show.
   Ginny is a ____.
4. Mary <u>writes</u> books.
   Mary is a ____.

Proper and Common Nouns, pages 48–49

Read each sentence. Write each noun. Write **proper**
if it is a proper noun. Write **common** if it is a
common noun.

1. Amy Gold rides her bike in Central Park.
2. A boy plays ball in the schoolyard.
3. Kevin walks his dog on Main Street.
4. Miss Yan bought a new car in June.
5. She drove the car to Arizona.

Writing Names, Addresses, and Dates, pages 50–54

Write each name and address correctly.

1.
```
jose rivera
29 hillside avenue
houston, texas 77039
```

3.
```
mr paul rosen
34 hudson street
portland, maine 04101
```

2.
```
dr anna feng
16 willow road
denver colorado 80220
```

4.
```
ms micco crow
46 maple drive
mobile alabama 36608
```

Write each date correctly.

5. june 3 1957
6. august 10 1962
7. march 12 1979
8. february 23 1978

9. october 8 1975
10. january 5 1981
11. april 2 1983
12. november 17 1982

Learning About Verbs, pages 70–71

Read each sentence. If the underlined word is a verb, write **verb.** If the underlined word is not a verb, write **not verb.**

1. Lee <u>reads</u> a book.
2. Randy turns the <u>pages</u>.
3. A boy <u>laughs</u> at a story.
4. Jake <u>jumps</u> rope.
5. Lisa turns the <u>rope</u>.
6. A dog <u>runs</u> by.

Verbs in Sentences, pages 72–73

Write each sentence. Underline the verb.

1. The girls play football.
2. Tom talks to the coach.
3. A man blows a whistle.
4. Carla kicks the ball.
5. The crowd cheers.
6. People jump up.

Verbs in the Present, pages 74–75

Read each sentence. Write **present** if the verb is in the present. Write **not present** if the verb is not.

1. Beth rides to the park.
2. A woman carries a baby.
3. Children played games.
4. A man sells balloons.
5. Two boys watch.
6. Jeff dropped the ball.

Using Verbs in the Present, pages 76–77

Write each sentence. Use the correct verb.

1. Sally ___ in the pool.   (swim, swims)
2. The boys ___ in the water.   (jump, jumps)
3. A girl ___ into the pool.   (dive, dives)
4. The girls ___ tag in the water.   (play, plays)

Spelling Verbs, pages 78–79

Write each sentence. Use the verb in the present.

1. Kim ___ a butterfly.   (chase)
2. Her sister ___ a net.   (carry)
3. Two boys ___ them.   (follow)
4. Roger ___ a frog.   (catch)
5. Two frogs ___ into the water.   (jump)
6. Roger ___ at them.   (laugh)

Verbs in the Past, pages 82–83

Read each sentence. Write **past** if the verb is in the past. Write **not past** if the verb is not.

1. Marc pumped the swing.
2. Paula pushes him.
3. My brother tossed a ball.
4. A boy runs to the field.
5. Angie picked some peas.
6. Diana washed the peas.

Spelling Verbs in the Past, pages 84--85

Write each sentence. Use the verb in the past.

1. Jimmy ___ to make a basket.   (learn)
2. Ronnie ___ the sofa.   (move)
3. The teacher ___ a funny movie.   (show)
4. A girl ___ to sing a song.   (try)
5. Inéz ___ the song.   (like)
6. Tom ___ me for his team.   (pick)

Three Kinds of Sentences, pages 108–109

Some special signs are missing in each sentence.
Write each sentence correctly.

1. the keeper feeds a tiger
2. A lion roars
3. did you hear the lion?
4. how loud it is!
5. two men clean the cages
6. a woman sells balloons.
7. did you buy a balloon
8. what a big balloon it is

Complete Sentences, pages 110–111

Write each sentence. Draw a line between the
subject part and the predicate part.

1. The girls went fishing.
2. Ming rowed the boat.
3. Sandy caught a big fish.
4. A girl made a fire.
5. Henry cooked the fish.
6. The children saved money.
7. Elena walked the dog.
8. The dog barked at a bird.

Nouns and Verbs in Sentences, pages 112–113

Write each sentence. Draw one line under each
noun. Draw two lines under each verb.

1. A boy wrote a story.
2. A girl painted a picture.
3. The class watched a movie.
4. The teacher laughed.
5. Some children played ball.
6. The woman sang a song.
7. A man played the piano.
8. The dancers bowed.

Pronouns in Sentences, pages 116–117

Look at the underlined words. Use the correct pronoun to take their place. Write the new sentence.

1. <u>Debra</u> picked some peas.
___ cooked them.

2. <u>The peas</u> are sweet.
___ taste good.

3. <u>Tom</u> picked apples.
___ baked a pie.

4. <u>The pie</u> is done.
___ is hot.

Using Pronouns in Sentences, pages 118–119

Use the correct verb in each sentence. Write the verb.

1. We ___ to school.   (walk, walks)
2. She ___ a car.   (drive, drives)
3. He ___ the bus.   (take, takes)
4. You ___ in a store.   (work, works)
5. I ___ on a farm.   (live, lives)
6. It ___ very tall.   (grow, grows)
7. They ___ us pick corn.   (help, helps)

Possessive Pronouns, pages 120–121

Write the second sentence using the correct pronoun.

1. Max paints houses.
___ painters work hard.

2. Max and I mix the paint.
___ hands get dirty.

3. Cindy wants a green door.
___ house is white.

4. The house is big.
___ doors are open.

Reviewing Nouns, pages 148–149

Read these sentences. Write each noun. Write
singular if the noun is singular. Write **plural** if the
noun is plural.

1. A girl picked flowers.
2. The boy saw a butterfly.
3. The butterfly had wings.
4. Two birds sang songs.
5. One bird flew fast.
6. A cat climbed a tree.
7. A turtle sat on a rock.
8. A cat saw the turtle.
9. Cats jumped on the rock.
10. Two dogs saw the cats.
11. A dog chased squirrels.
12. A squirrel ran up a tree.

Read each sentence. Write each noun. Write **proper**
if the noun is a proper noun. Write **common** if the
noun is a common noun.

1. Andy went to the park.
2. Mrs. Smith drove a bus.
3. Bill lives on Wax Road.
4. The bus stopped.
5. Did Mary get on the bus?
6. Don ran in the woods.
7. Mr. Ray led the hike.
8. A girl found a nest.
9. Did Lee see the nest?
10. Carl and Mandy raced.

Write each sentence correctly. Use a capital letter
to begin each important word in a proper noun.

1. pam planted a garden.
2. miss gomez helped.
3. sue went to lake school.
4. john pulled the weeds.
5. bob watered the lawn.
6. peter sold roses to ann.
7. mrs. fine bought some.
8. juan lives on oak road.
9. fisher hall is big.
10. joe cut the grass.

Looking at Possessive Nouns, pages 150–155

Decide if the noun in ( ) is singular or plural. Then
use the possessive form of the noun in the blank.
Write the sentence.

1. The ___ cat had kittens.   (girls)
2. Kurt lost his ___ ball.   (friend)
3. He looked in the ___ box.   (cat)
4. The ___ ball belonged to Roy.   (kittens)

Possessive Nouns with Special Endings, pages 158–159

Look at the noun in ( ). Use the possessive form of
the noun in the blank. Write the sentence.

1. The ___ cat cries.   (child)
2. I saw the ___ car.   (men)
3. We saw ___ tails.   (mice)
4. The ___ hat fell.   (man)

Writing Sentences, page 160

Read each pair of sentences. Put them together to
make one sentence. Write the new sentence.

1. Brenda has a cat.
   The cat has kittens.

2. Jill keeps mice.
   The mice live in cages.

3. The boys have a dog.
   The dog runs quickly.

4. The girls walk their dog.
   The dog pulls them along.

Writing Days, Months, and Special Days, pages 162–163

Write each sentence. Use capital letters correctly.

1. This monday is halloween.
2. Does august begin today?
3. We played on saturday.
4. Today is new year's day.

Adjectives, pages 184–187

Read each sentence. Write the adjective. Then write the noun it describes.

1. There is a tall tree.
2. A gray squirrel climbs.
3. It has a bushy tail.
4. A big bird flies away.
5. It has a yellow beak.
6. I found a smooth stone.
7. I dropped a shiny coin.
8. We felt the cold water.
9. An orange fish swam by.
10. A little girl sat down.

Adjectives That Compare, pages 188–189

Choose the correct adjective to fill each blank. Then write the sentence.

1. Rosa saved old baseball cards.
   Jorge had an ___ card than Rosa's.   (older, oldest)
2. Mark found the ___ card of all.   (older, oldest)
3. We took a long walk.
   Pam took a ___ walk than ours.   (longer, longest)
4. Paul took the ___ walk of all.   (longer, longest)

Number Words, page 190

Complete each sentence with a number word. Write the sentence.

1. I saw ___ skateboards.
2. I counted ___ bicycles.
3. ___ people played ball.
4. ___ boy rode a horse.
5. ___ children flew kites.
6. A girl sailed ___ boat.
7. ___ dogs chased a cat.
8. ___ man chased the dogs.

Articles, page 191

Complete each sentence. Use a correct article.
Write the sentence.

1. I have ____ bicycle.

2. My aunt has ____ orange.

3. We ride down ____ street.

4. Sara eats ____ apple.

5. ____ apples grow on trees.

6. We have ____ big basket.

Words with the Same Meaning, page 194

Read each sentence. Write a synonym for the
underlined word.

1. Beth is a <u>nice</u> person.

2. She makes <u>pretty</u> hats.

3. Jon is a very <u>smart</u> boy.

4. A <u>big</u> dog barked.

5. An <u>unhappy</u> baby cried.

6. The <u>noisy</u> child yelled.

Words with Opposite Meanings, page 195

Use an antonym for the underlined word. Write the
new sentence.

1. I had an <u>open</u> umbrella.

2. She wore an <u>old</u> coat.

3. I took off my <u>wet</u> shoes.

4. I need a <u>soft</u> pillow.

5. I am a <u>slow</u> worker.

6. He sewed a <u>new</u> pillow.

Making Adjectives, pages 196–197

Make the word in ( ) into an adjective. Complete the
sentence with the adjective. Write the sentence.

1. I have a ____ cat.   (fur)

2. I saw a ____ hill.   (rock)

3. It was a ____ day.   (sun)

4. We wore ____ boots.   (dust)

Verbs in the Present and Past, pages 220–221

Use the correct verb in the present. Write the sentence.

1. Dan ___ home. (rush)

2. He ___ hard. (try)

3. A friend ___ by. (pass)

4. Joan ___ her bike. (fix)

5. She ___ Toby. (race)

6. Toby ___ fast. (ride)

Use the correct verb in the past. Write the sentence.

1. We ___ tennis. (play)

2. I ___ the ball. (toss)

3. You ___ to it. (race)

4. They ___ later. (watch)

5. A player ___. (kick)

6. You ___ then. (worry)

Verbs in the Future, pages 222–223

Write each verb. Then write whether each verb is in the **present,** the **past,** or the **future.**

1. Joan raced today.

2. She will race later.

3. Joan runs fast.

4. Todd will swim today.

5. He won a race earlier.

6. Todd swims well.

Using Verbs in the Past, pages 224–225

Write the verb that names an action in the past.

1. The dogs ___ home. (go)

2. They ___ a meal. (eat)

3. A girl ___ them. (see)

4. The boys ___ not. (do)

5. They ___ away. (go)

6. I ___ a bone to one. (give)

7. My cat ___ fast. (grow)

8. I ___ your friend. (know)

9. The cat ___ a nap. (take)

10. The dog ___ to bark. (begin)

Helping Verbs, pages 226–227

Write the helping verb and the verb.

1. We have played ball.
2. You have enjoyed it.
3. Sue has improved a lot.
4. Ed has started a team.
5. They have walked away.
6. Brian has talked to me.
7. I have joined.
8. Kim has thanked me.
9. They have wanted players.
10. We have learned a lot.

More Verbs in the Past, pages 228–229

Complete each sentence. Write the correct form of the verb.

1. Margie has ___ to the zoo.   (go)
2. She has ___ many wild animals.   (see)
3. Many birds have ___ past her.   (fly)
4. A little brown monkey has ___ a banana.   (take)
5. Margie has ___ to feel tired.   (begin)
6. She has ___ all her lunch.   (eat)

Contractions, pages 232–233

Write each sentence using a contraction for the underlined words.

1. I <u>can</u> <u>not</u> swim in deep water.
2. He <u>does</u> <u>not</u> like cold water.
3. Our friends <u>do</u> <u>not</u> want to race.
4. A little girl <u>did</u> <u>not</u> stay.
5. She <u>has</u> <u>not</u> learned to swim yet.
6. We <u>have</u> <u>not</u> been at the pool all day.

Three Kinds of Sentences, pages 256–257

Write each sentence correctly. Then write **telling** if it is a telling sentence. Write **question** if it a question sentence. Write **exclamation** if it is an exclamation sentence.

1. Did you see the movie
2. a dog was the star.
3. the dog did tricks
4. did your sister laugh?

5. what a funny laugh it was!
6. Did the dog bark
7. How loud the barking was
8. did you like the movie?

Nouns and Pronouns in the Subject Part, pages 258–259

Write the main word in the subject part. Write **noun** if the word is a noun. Write **pronoun** if the word is a pronoun.

1. The birds sing songs.
2. Father likes to sing.
3. He made up a song.
4. I sang with him.

5. Mother laughed.
6. She did a little dance.
7. A neighbor joined us.
8. We danced around.

Verbs in Sentences, pages 260–261

Write each sentence. Underline the verb.

1. I went to a party.
2. Gail made my costume.
3. She painted a paper bag.
4. She cut two holes in it.

5. I made funny noises.
6. My friends laughed.
7. We played games.
8. We enjoyed the party.

Building Sentences, pages 262–263

Add words to the subject part and predicate part of each sentence. Then write the sentence.

1. The window broke.
2. A man shouted.
3. The children ran.
4. A baby cried.
5. Dogs barked.

6. The snow fell.
7. The boys played.
8. Mother called.
9. The sun set.
10. An owl hooted.

Understanding New Words, pages 264–265

Read each sentence. Write the underlined word in each sentence. Write what you think the word means.

1. Becky had an <u>accident</u>.
   She fell down the stairs.
2. The shirt was a <u>bargain</u>.
   It was on sale.
3. Rico has a good <u>imagination</u>.
   He pretends he can fly.
4. My sister is a <u>member</u> of the Girl Scouts.
   She belongs to Troop 23.
5. Many apple trees grow in the <u>orchard</u>.
6. I <u>shiver</u> in the cold rain.
7. We used an <u>oar</u> to row the boat.
8. The apartment is <u>vacant</u>.
   The family moved out.

INDEX